MINI HABITS FOR TEENS

MINI HABITS FOR TEENS

Small Changes
to Help You
Navigate Life's
Challenges

Kate Gladdin

ROCKRIDGE
PRESS

For general information on our other products and services or to obtain technical support, please contact our Customer Care Department within the United States at (866) 744-2665, or outside the United States at (510) 253-0500.

Rockridge Press publishes its books in a variety of electronic and print formats. Some content that appears in print may not be available in electronic books, and vice versa.

TRADEMARKS: Rockridge Press and the Rockridge Press logo are trademarks or registered trademarks of Callisto Media Inc. and/or its affiliates, in the United States and other countries, and may not be used without written permission. All other trademarks are the property of their respective owners. Rockridge Press is not associated with any product or vendor mentioned in this book.

Interior and Cover Designer: Emma Hall
Art Producer: Samantha Ulban
Editor: John Makowski
Production Editor: Ruth Sakata Corley
Production Manager: Martin Worthington

All images used under license Shutterstock. Author photo courtesy of Princeton Headshots.

ISBN: Print 978-1-64876-948-1
eBook 978-1-64876-949-8
R0

To my Pop
and your wise words
that are always with me:
"Work hard and do what
makes you happy, Love."

CONTENTS

INTRODUCTION

"There's just too much to get done!" Audrey, one of my coaching clients, sobbed to me at the beginning of one of our sessions. She was trying to pack for her move to college and felt completely overwhelmed by it. I could almost feel the weight of the heavy thoughts racing through her mind.

Do you ever feel the same? I know I did as a teen. Growing up is tough. It can feel like the older you get, the more responsibilities and expectations fall on you. More and more, adults tell you "be more like this," "do less of that," "try harder," "be more respectful," "manage your time better," and "don't be so lazy!"

Yeah, I didn't enjoy adults telling me what to do as a teen either. This isn't that kind of book. I'm not going to try to teach you things you *have* to do. But I will share with you ideas and habits that you can *choose* to practice if you want to make your path through school and your life beyond it easier, more interesting, and rewarding! It might not seem like it, but the little things you get into the habit of doing now can completely alter the direction of your life down the track.

I know this because it was the habit of practicing gratitude daily that gave me the strength I needed to cope with the sudden loss of my sister when I was just 20 years old. It was the habit of exercising daily that set me on a path toward winning an Australian fitness title two years later. And it was the habit of making to-do lists that gave me the organizational skills I needed to begin running my own speaking business a couple of years after that. What you do today has an impact on tomorrow: It can either take you further from your goals or closer to them. This book is filled with tips you can use to set yourself up for success in all key areas of your life, now and in the future.

And don't just take my word for it: Students I've coached have found the confidence to make new friendships and land roles in school musicals through practicing the habits in chapter 3. Other teen clients have made the cross-country team and achieved their goal grades through applying the habits in chapter 5. Some have gone from constantly arguing with their moms to having a loving and fun relationship with them by committing to the habits in chapter 6. Audrey ended up leaving that session smiling and excited to get packing for college because I shared with her some of the mini habits in chapter 4. And now I'd love to help you achieve the same kind of success!

I am honored to become your life coach. Throughout this book we'll explore the most important habits you can start practicing to take life into your own hands, feel more emotionally resilient, and turn goal setting into goal getting. All I ask is that you keep an open mind and trust in the process. These mini habits may seem insignificant, but once you get momentum going with them, you'll be amazed at the difference they can make in your overall fulfillment and happiness in life.

One last thing: I may call myself a "life coach," but please know I'm human just like you and still a work in progress myself. So think of me as a peer who's just a few steps ahead of you on this wild journey called life. And although at times we'll get deep and meaningful, know that we're going to have fun whenever we can throughout this book. Losing my sister so young taught me life is too short not to go after your goals and enjoy yourself along the way. So, let's begin!

How to Use This Book

You probably know that simply reading about these mini habits isn't enough—applying them is what will change your life. I know it can feel overwhelming to try changing everything at once, so this book is organized in bite-size chapters that focus on specific key areas of your life. You can step your way through at your own pace. We cover it all in this book, one by one and strategy by strategy, from relationships to social skills to personal health to time management to goal setting. The tools you'll learn to use are powerful individually; in combination they're your ultimate road map to improving your ability to navigate challenges and thrive in life!

To get the most out of this book, I recommend reading it the whole way through in the order it's written. However, you can skip around a little if you first want to learn about a particular area you're struggling with. As a bonus tip, to really absorb and apply what you learn from this book, read it with a highlighter in hand. As you go, highlight your favorite quotes or the lessons you enjoy most so those sections will jump out at you instantly whenever you need a refresher on what was shared. Or, if you don't like to mark your books, grab yourself a notebook or open a note-taking app on your phone and make notes on the parts that you find most helpful, so you can easily look back at them anytime you need a boost of guidance or inspiration. Either way, know that this book and my words will always be here for you!

Part One

THE WORD ON HABITS

Welcome to part 1 of this book! I'm excited to dive into all things "habits" with you. Although you're holding this book in your hands, perhaps you're not too sure what a habit actually is or why habits matter so much. In this section, we explore the science of habits and how they impact so many different areas of our lives, so you'll realize that this book is definitely worth reading! We also discuss helpful versus unhelpful habits and how to recognize them in your own life.

Chapter One

LET'S TALK HABITS

Buckle up and get ready to officially take off into the world of habits! First, we'll explore the basics of what a habit is and the three steps involved in forming one. This will help you understand what causes your behavior to turn from something you do once to something you repeat all the time. (It's really fascinating!) Then we'll turn our attention to all the different areas of your life that habits can affect, including personal health, relationships, social skills, and academic achievement.

What Are Habits?

What do brushing your teeth, checking social media, practicing basketball daily, and biting your nails all have in common? They're all habits. Some of them are helpful, some not so much, but all are simple examples of what a habit is: routine behavior that we do regularly. Research has found that about 40 percent of your day is made up of habitual behavior.

Our habits can take effort to put into place initially, but once we've repeated a specific action enough times, it becomes a memorized pattern of behavior in our brain that we do almost effortlessly. For example, when we were learning to dress ourselves, at first even putting our own shirt on was a bit of a struggle. We had to consciously think about where to put our arms and how to line up the sleeves. But now I bet you can do it automatically with your eyes closed. That's a sign of a habit. Sometimes we've repeated a habit so often that we don't even realize we're doing it.

The key thing to understand about habits is that they don't just happen. They're built through repetition of the same specific behavior over and over.

The Three Steps of Forming Habits

Our habits are as unique as we are. Yet despite their uniqueness, there is a three-step process that scientists have found is part of every single habit. It's called "the habit loop," and it includes a cue, a behavior, and a reward. Once you understand how you form a habit, you can learn how to get unstuck from your bad habits and make your good habits stick!

THE CUE

A cue is the stimulus that triggers your brain to perform a particular habit. Cues can be found all around us all day, every day, and typically fit into five main categories: time, place, feelings, other people, or the action that you just took. Anything from getting a text notification, walking past your kitchen, feeling anxious, or finding somewhere to sit at lunch can be considered a cue that your brain has learned a routine response to because it has repeated that behavior many times before. For example, seeing a mirror can be a cue for you to check your hair.

THE BEHAVIOR

The behavior is the "action part" of your habit—the response to the stimulus of the cue—which, if repeated often enough, can become an automatic reaction. Perhaps you instantly check your phone as soon as you hear the notification buzz. That's cue behavior in action. Without paying attention, you instantly scroll through your phone because the cue of the notification triggered that memorized response.

For me, walking into the kitchen (the cue) is a trigger for me to check my fridge for a snack (the behavior). Feeling anxious (the cue) can trigger you to pick at your cuticles (the behavior). Even thoughts can be a response to a cue. For example, looking for somewhere to sit at lunch (the cue) can trigger you to have the habitual thought "No one wants to talk to me" or "I'm always left out."

Our thoughts aren't actions we take out there in the world; they are "actions we take in our mind" that directly influence our behavior in the world. Throughout this book we'll pay attention to our habitual thoughts as well as our actions.

THE REWARD

Our brains seek to do things that give positive reinforcement and feel satisfying and worthwhile. That's why the behavior must end in some sort of "reward" that feels good to us in order for us to want to repeat it often enough to become a habit.

The reward could be the satisfying taste of your afternoon cookie, the relief you feel from hiding in the corner at lunch so you don't have to speak to anyone, or the sense of pride you get from reading another chapter in your book before bed. If there's no end reward for your behavior, your brain won't be motivated to repeat it. The reward is key in making your behavior a habit.

To piece it all together, there's a cue that triggers a specific behavior that results in a reward that then prompts your brain to want to repeat the behavior the next time it comes across that cue. As one example, eyeing the chips in your kitchen cupboard triggers you to eat the bag of chips (the behavior) that then gives you the satisfaction of taste and pleasure (the reward). Over time, this habit loop—cue, behavior, reward—becomes more ingrained in your brain. The habit becomes automatic, and you can actually begin to crave the reward that comes from performing it.

How Habits Affect Us

How healthy we are—inside and out—doesn't happen randomly; it happens through our habits. What we consistently do over and over is either going to take us closer to or further away from our goals. This book is all about forming the habits that bring you closer to your goals in all areas of your life.

EMOTIONAL WELL-BEING

Would you like to feel less stressed and more in control of your emotions on a daily basis? Well, your habits are a great way to do that! Some of us grow up learning unhelpful habits to deal with our negative emotions, like trying to push them away or judging ourselves for having them, which actually only adds to the intensity of those feelings. Sometimes we'll have a habit of overeating or spending hours watching Netflix to try to escape those emotions. These habits of trying to resist or escape our emotions only take away from our emotional well-being and often leave us feeling even worse. The good news is that forming habits that are the opposite of these can do the reverse! There's no better feeling than knowing how to look after yourself emotionally even when life gets challenging.

PHYSICAL WELL-BEING

From keeping our heart beating 4,800 times an hour to producing 300 billion new cells every single day without us even realizing it, our bodies are beyond incredible! Yet we often don't treat them that way. For example, in a world where there's a lot of delicious food to eat and fun things to do without having to leave the couch, it's easy to get into the habit of overeating and under-exercising. The impacts of this on our physical well-being can add up quickly.

Committing to healthier habits can help you feel stronger, have clearer skin, boost your energy levels, sleep better, be faster and fitter in sports, and overall feel more comfortable with yourself! That's why making an effort toward instilling healthy habits is so worthwhile. Feeling great in your body is a reward money can't buy!

MENTAL WELL-BEING

Life's pressures can make it easy to let negative thinking take over and keep us ruminating, stuck in thinking about things that go wrong. If we let this become our default response to challenges, it can take a real toll on our mental well-being and even lead to conditions like depression and anxiety.

Mental well-being doesn't mean you think and feel positive *all* of the time. That's not realistic or necessary. It's perfectly healthy, and sometimes even helpful, to occasionally feel disappointed or hurt as you process an experience. Due to our ancestors' needs to always be aware of threats, our brains have developed a negativity bias—so it's normal to have automatic negative thoughts (or ANTs) spring up in different situations every day. You always have the ability to create daily habits that help you manage those ANTs and boost your mental well-being big time!

The Effect of Habits

RELATIONSHIPS

From always texting your friends a nice message on their birthdays to thanking your mom when she brings your folded laundry into your room, there are habits that can really help our relationships grow and thrive. However, it's easy for life to get so busy that you forget to check in on a friend you haven't spoken to in a while or not bother to thank your dad when he picks you up late after practice.

In the long term, the lack of effort and care we're showing can really begin to erode our relationships, even with those who mean the most to us. Maybe you're in the habit of being quite sarcastic or short-tempered with your parents, and this creates tension in your relationship. The solution is building simple habits that help you show up as the kind of friend, son, daughter, sibling, student, or teammate you want to be so you can strengthen your relationships. That's exactly what we'll explore together in chapter 6.

SOCIAL SKILLS

The tendency to mumble, worry over what someone is thinking of you, or interrupt a friend mid-sentence to say something that just popped into your head are all examples of habits that can hold you back in social situations. Whether or not you're aware of them, everything from your body language and tone of voice to your style of listening and level of confidence impacts your ability to communicate and connect with others.

Perhaps you believe you "just are" socially awkward, but the truth is this kind of awkwardness comes from habitual behavior that you can change on purpose by creating new habits. In chapter 3, you'll learn simple yet powerful habits you can practice to begin to build up your social skills so you not only speak with more confidence but also listen with more empathy. That's when you'll finally find the courage to do things like talk to your crush, audition for the school play, or be there for your friend when they need someone to confide in.

SCHOOL

Are your grades not where you want them to be because you forget to do your homework or always leave your assignments till the last minute? Well, you're not alone. Research has found that 86 percent of high school students struggle with the habit of procrastination. Although scrolling TikTok rather than finishing your math homework feels good in the moment, the downside to procrastinating is that it often leaves us with more work to do and less time to do it. Then we're left feeling overwhelmed and unable to do the tasks to the best of our abilities.

If you want to improve your grades, reduce your stress, and stop your parents nagging you so much about your schoolwork, then chapter 4 is for you! It's packed with the best time-management practices to replace the habit of procrastination with ones that'll help you be way more productive and organized so you can get results you're proud of.

PERSONAL HEALTH

Do you tend to feel sluggish from going to bed too late? Or do you sometimes feel caught in a negative mindset that you can't seem to get out of? These are signs that your personal health could do with a boost from new habits that better support your mental, emotional, and physical well-being. In chapter 5, I'll share some simple changes in your routine that can reap huge rewards for your mind, body, and spirit.

Most teens I coach tell me they typically go to bed around 2 a.m. because they're up playing video games, surfing the internet, or chatting with friends online. These may seem like harmless activities, but your amazing brain actually needs around 8 to 10 hours of sleep to keep up with the important changes it's making during this phase in your life; otherwise, your energy levels and mindset will suffer. So while it can be tough to kick the habit of staying up and using your phone or laptop, it's tougher in the long term not to. Chronic sleep deprivation can lead to mental health conditions, like depression.

LONG-TERM GOALS

What's one thing you want to achieve by a year from now? Is it making it onto the soccer team? Having a B+ average across all classes? Saving $500 from doing your chores or getting your first job? Whatever your goal is, I'm going to share the secret to achieving it: building good habits that support the goal you're striving for. What you do consistently is what creates progress, and progress is what brings you closer to your goal.

Think of it like a wooden carving. There's no one magic stroke that creates it. Instead, it takes hundreds of strokes chipping away at the wood to turn it into a masterpiece. The same goes with our goals: The daily chipping away that can feel pointless in the beginning actually makes the progress you need to turn your goal setting into goal getting!

Takeaways

We've explored a lot about habits this chapter, so let's do a quick recap of the key takeaways:

- A habit is routine behavior we do automatically.
- There are three steps to the process of forming a habit: a cue, a trigger, and a reward.
- Habits impact every area of our life, from our achievements to our friendships to our physical fitness.
- If we want to improve a specific area of our lives, we need to look at which habits we need to change for the better.

Chapter Two

START SMALL

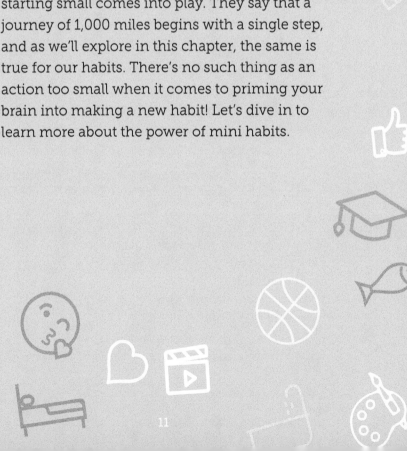

It's easy to feel overwhelmed when starting out with a new habit. That's where the power of starting small comes into play. They say that a journey of 1,000 miles begins with a single step, and as we'll explore in this chapter, the same is true for our habits. There's no such thing as an action too small when it comes to priming your brain into making a new habit! Let's dive in to learn more about the power of mini habits.

Set Your Goals

What's a good goal to have? What should it look like? How big should I go? Truthfully, the answer to all those questions is that it's entirely up to you. There's no right or wrong goal to have, but it is important to pick goals that matter to you and help you become a better version of yourself.

It's also helpful to split your goals into two categories: short-term and long-term goals. It's awesome to have a long-term vision of where you want to end up, but sometimes a long-term goal can just feel so big that it's overwhelming to get started. That's why it's powerful to also set short-term goals. Short-term goals can feel more manageable and help us build the skills and self-confidence needed to reach our long-term goals. Let's explore some examples of the kinds of goals you might want to achieve!

SHORT-TERM GOALS

Short-term goals are anything that you want to achieve in the immediate future, whether that's this week, next month, by the end of the semester, or within the next year. They can go beyond grades to revolve around your social life, sports ambitions, well-being, hobbies, family relationships, or desire for more independence in the world. Here are some examples:

- Get onto the team of my chosen sport
- Hand in my resume to five local stores
- Pass science class
- Run my first 5K
- Make a new friend at school
- Get a B average for all subjects
- Land a role in the school musical
- Talk to my crush

Find a tutor for math

Get my average daily screen time on my phone to
2 hours or less

Fight less often with my siblings

Eat less sugar each day

Read 20 books this year

LONG-TERM GOALS

Long-term goals are the things you want to achieve beyond
the next 12 months: deciding what college you want to
get into or where you'd like to work over the summer.
Long-term goals could include things that are so far away
that your brain just tells you, "I don't know." Challenge yourself to stay open-minded and have some fun brainstorming
goals you'd like to have ticked off in the next two, three, or
five years. Here are some more examples for you:

Get at least 1100 on the SATs

Choose a college I want to apply to

Save my first $2,000

Be the leader of the student council

Run my first half marathon

Submit my creative writing to the Young
Writers Awards

Get my first casual job

Have 500 subscribers to my YouTube channel

Make the varsity football team

Intern as a graphic designer over the summer

Have a close and healthy relationship with my dad

Only eat takeout food once a month

Be captain of my soccer team

DISCOVER YOUR GOALS!

Grab a notebook and a pen, or open up a fresh doc on your computer or in a note-taking app on your phone, and let's begin choosing the best goals for you. We'll start with a long-term goal.

1. **Think about yourself two years from now. What's *one thing* you want to be able to say you've achieved?**

   Write down whatever answer comes to mind for you! Don't pick the one that you feel like you "should" go after but the one that really stands out to you and you'd feel pumped about having achieved for yourself.

   Now, we're going to dial in your focus and choose a short-term goal.

2. **What's one *thing* you'll feel proud of yourself for achieving three months from now?**

   If we make our goal too vague (like "get a good grade"), it's hard to stay motivated because we don't really know what we're aiming for. The more clearly and specifically we can state our goals—what we want to happen and when—the more laser-focused we'll be on exactly what habits we need to get us to that goal. And we'll be able to measure our progress along the way to ensure we're on track!

Why Mini Habits?

Mini habits are like jelly beans. They're bite-size positive changes in behavior that we use to get momentum going toward our goal. The human brain isn't motivated to do hard things. So trying to convince it to do something challenging that it's not used to, like going for a five-mile run when you've never run a mile before, isn't realistic. Your brain will throw a little "I can't be bothered" tantrum and give you every reason not to do it.

That's why we have to almost trick our brain into building better habits by starting small, coaxing it toward the positive change with baby steps. This makes it easier to follow through on the desired action, which is important when forming a habit. When you say, "I will do X," and then you do X, your brain gets a good hit of the reward chemical dopamine. Your brain seeks this in order to memorize that behavior as a habit.

For example, rather than aiming to run five miles every day, run around your block each day. As you begin to take the consistent action of running around the block every day, you begin to build the habits and identity of a runner, someone who always does those things. From there, it's easier to begin to increase the duration or intensity of your habit.

Making Mini Habits Stick

We may have taken the new positive action once or twice, but then we find we're back to the same habit of sleeping in or forgetting to journal in our diaries. It's easy at this point to feel deflated and give up entirely. But you don't have to! What you're feeling is part of the process. Installing new habits does take extra energy and commitment *temporarily*, but here are some tips to make it easier:

- Be realistic with the time you have available. If you want to study three hours each night but don't usually get home from basketball practice until 8 p.m., then it's not fair or healthy to stay up studying so late. Ask yourself, "What's a fair amount to study that doesn't compromise my well-being or other goals?"
- Showing up and following through on what you said you were going to do is a skill that will serve you well in *all* areas of your life and future career, so don't get too caught up in how fast you ran or how far you got with the essay during your homework. Appreciate yourself for the fact you stuck to your commitments and showed up for yourself—even when it was hard!
- Beware of the inner critic who tells you that you can't do it. Your brain's default mode is to be lazy and not want to change, but know that you can override that and speak back to those negative thoughts. Here are some of my favorite positive thoughts:
  - "I can figure this out!"
  - "It's not about how well I do it. It just matters that I do it—every action counts!"
  - "I am proud of you. Even if today didn't go as planned, tomorrow is a new day to make progress!"

Takeaways

Setting goals is an important part of deciding what habits we want to instill in our lives.

Short-term goals are ones you want to achieve in the next 12 months. Long-term goals are anything you want to achieve beyond that.

Starting small with mini habits will make it easier for our brain to get started on taking action and feel the reward of following through. This helps build our self-esteem and identity as someone who *can* do these things.

Part Two

MAKE IT A (MINI) HABIT

Now that we've arrived at part 2 of this book, we'll take a deep dive into the specific areas we're going to work on for setting up and strengthening your mini habits. From building confidence to getting better sleep to budgeting and creating happier relationships, this section will teach you the best habits to set you up for greater success in life.

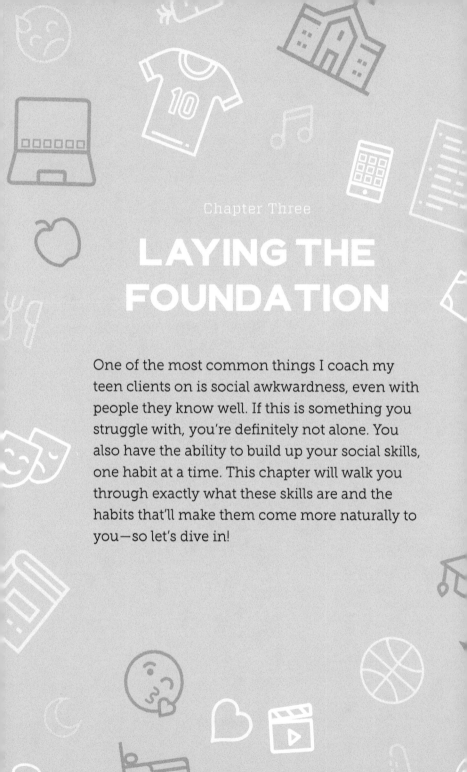

Chapter Three

LAYING THE FOUNDATION

One of the most common things I coach my teen clients on is social awkwardness, even with people they know well. If this is something you struggle with, you're definitely not alone. You also have the ability to build up your social skills, one habit at a time. This chapter will walk you through exactly what these skills are and the habits that'll make them come more naturally to you—so let's dive in!

People Skills

It's totally normal to feel socially awkward sometimes, especially when you're a tween or teen. You're going through a lot of changes that can make it challenging to feel comfortable in your own skin. Trying to figure out what you like and who you really are can feel messy. However, developing your people skills (aka social skills) is one of the most important aspects of building all other healthy habits. At our core, we are a social species and thrive most in life when we're feeling connected to and well supported by those around us. Plus, nearly every goal you'll want to pursue requires communication skills that rely on the following key elements.

CONFIDENCE

Many of us try to build our self-confidence based on external things like our grades, appearance, friends' opinions, parents' praise, or how many followers we have on social media. It's not wrong to seek validation from those things. But it does get exhausting and can cause a lot of anxiety as we become afraid of failure, judgment, and rejection—all of which are inevitable parts of everyday life!

Instead, true self-confidence comes from understanding that our worth as human beings is something that is inherent in us, and nothing in the world can take that away. You are 100 percent worthy just as you are. If you find that challenging to believe right now, that's okay! We all have a critic in our mind who tends to get us in the habit of noticing what's wrong with us and fearing other people are going to think the same. When we believe the myths our inner critic tells us, we tend to get into the habit of hiding away from others who might judge us, and our social life suffers.

EMOTIONAL AWARENESS

Imagine how you would act toward a friend when you're feeling excited to see them versus how you would act when you're feeling upset at something they've just said. You'd probably use a different tone of voice and body language. Our feelings drive our behavior. If we want to get a handle on our emotional reactions to situations, we need to become more aware of what we're feeling and why we're feeling that way. Often, the source of our feelings is different from what we initially think it is. For example, I grew up believing my feelings were caused by what happened to me. In this section, we're going to dive into the true cause of our emotions. This is one of the most important lessons you can learn to feel less helpless and more in control of your emotional life, no matter what difficult circumstances you might face.

NONVERBAL CUES

Have you ever sensed that your sibling was upset or your friend was anxious, without them even saying a word? Perhaps they were slouched over on the kitchen table with their head in their hands or were looking away and fidgeting with their pocket when you were talking to them. These are nonverbal cues, which are essentially communication that happens without spoken words. You're interpreting nonverbal cues every day without even noticing. In fact, research has found that about 70 percent of our daily communication happens nonverbally—think tone of voice, body language, eye contact, and facial expressions.

Developing our awareness of other people's nonverbal cues is important for becoming more socially skilled. But we also need to be more mindful of how our own cues, especially body language and eye contact, could be coming across to someone else. Most of our nonverbal cues happen automatically, but we can learn how to monitor them to adapt to different social settings and show respect toward others, as we'd like them to do for us. In doing so, our social interactions become far more rewarding!

ACTIVE LISTENING

Think about a time when you were trying to tell your friend about something important to you—like how you'd just spoken to your crush or that you're stressed about the exam next week—and the whole time they were just scrolling on their phone and paying zero attention to you. How did it feel? Probably not awesome, right? No one likes the feeling of not being heard. Yet with so many things grabbing at our attention these days, we're easily distracted. That's why active listening is an important part of being a good friend, student, teammate, sibling, and son or daughter: It helps people feel valued because we're showing them that we care and they're worth listening to.

EMPATHY

Empathy is the ability to put yourself in someone else's shoes and try to imagine how they're thinking and feeling. It's a powerful way to connect to people and build more trust and understanding in our relationships. Separate from sympathy, which is feeling sorry for someone, empathy is a more direct line to "I feel you." Even if we haven't gone through the exact same experience as someone else, we know what it's like to feel helpless, overwhelmed, or dis-appointed. We all have the ability to practice empathy to help others feel better understood and less alone in this big wide world.

Confidence

Not to be confused with arrogance, which is "I'm better than you," confidence is about embracing who you really are and embracing others for who they really are. It's about knowing that there's no "better than" because we're all amazing in our own unique way!

The trouble is, our brain has a habit of being super self-critical and constantly comparing other people's abilities, achievements, or appearances with our own. This leads us to constantly feeling "less than." We begin to look outside of ourselves for approval and can become hooked on getting other people to like and validate us so we can feel better about ourselves.

This leads to a fragile self-esteem because you're always dependent on someone or something else to make you feel exactly how you want to feel, and that's simply unrealistic. Inevitably, you'll make mistakes, be rejected, fail at things, or interact with people who dislike you. And that's all okay. True self-confidence is owning that your opinion of yourself is the opinion that matters most!

Instead of fearing mistakes, failures, and rejection as fatal to your success and feeling like your abilities are set in concrete (aka a "fixed mindset"), you can develop a "growth mindset," a term coined by psychologist Carol Dweck. A growth mindset purposely allows room for failures, mistakes, and other people judging you poorly. People with a growth mindset understand that every time they mess up, they have an opportunity to learn something and improve their abilities so they can do better next time. There is no true failure, unless you failed to try at all.

Of course, it takes courage to try something new or put yourself in a position for others to judge you. To follow through in spite of this, you'll want to get clear on your own values and what you want to stand for in the world. Then you can commit to acting in alignment with your values no matter the emotional discomfort it may sometimes cause.

When you build your self-confidence around honoring your values and being proud of who you are, not just what you're achieving, you'll be amazed at what you're willing to pursue. Failure and rejection don't take away your worth. In fact, the lessons you learn from those experiences actually help you bring more of your worth into the world.

Whether or not someone likes you is beyond your control. When we focus on what we can't control, we may feel anxious. Instead, flip the question to focus on what you do have control over: "What do I like about them?"

Focusing on what's within our control feels way more empowering, and making it a priority to discover something cool or interesting about someone else works in your favor—people love people who show interest in them. It's a win-win!

To bring this back to forming habits, the next time "Do they like me?" pops into your head (the cue), use that as a *trigger* to redirect your mind to the powerful question "What do I like about them?" (the behavior). Then, feel your anxiety subside a little as you relax into the conversation you began by getting curious about them (the reward).

Because of our ANTs (see page 7), many of our beliefs are self-critical and negative. So we have to purposely instruct our brain to find proof that shows we are amazing and capable just the way we are!

In a journal, or on a fresh piece of paper or a blank page on your phone or computer, write or type at the top the following heading: "I am enough the way I am. I know this because . . ."

For the next 60 days, you're going to purposely search for evidence from your daily life or your past that proves that you add value to this world just the way you are! Write down each of those things every day. There's no proof too small to be included on this list—it could be any little thing you do or notice about yourself during the day. To ensure this becomes a habit, put this list somewhere visible and make it a point to add to it at a specific time of day after doing something that's already a habit for you, like brushing your teeth.

To build your resilience to failure and feel more confident putting yourself out there even when the outcome isn't guaranteed, celebrate yourself for your "Worthy Failure of the Week"—an action you took that's aligned with your values but didn't necessarily turn out in your favor. We want to get into the habit of celebrating those actions because you were successful in acting according to your values and desires, even when you felt afraid. True failure would be to let those fears get in the way and take no action at all.

On a whiteboard in your bedroom (or on a big piece of paper to stick up on your wall), write the heading "Worthy Failure of the Week." Set a reminder on your phone to go off every Friday afternoon after your last class to reflect on the week and write down one worthy failure from the last seven days.

Emotional Awareness

Emotional awareness is the ability to recognize your own feelings, what causes them, and healthy ways to handle them that don't jeopardize your relationship with yourself or other people. A big part of this is understanding that people or circumstances don't cause our feelings.

As Holocaust survivor and psychiatrist Dr. Viktor Frankl once said, "Between stimulus and response there is a space, and in that space lies our greatest power." The space he is talking about here is our mind. Our own thinking—not what's happening outside of us—creates our feelings. We know this is true because if circumstances themselves caused our feelings, then we'd all have the exact same experience of them. We don't, because we all interpret things differently.

While we can't always change the things that are happening outside of us, we always have the power to change the way we think about and interpret things. We are never helpless when it comes to how we feel and react. This means we need to practice greater self-awareness to step out of blame mode and take responsibility for our own emotions. We need to intentionally choose our response to things rather than freaking out in automatic reactions.

It's perfectly okay to feel however you feel, but understand you can choose to let thoughts pass through your mind without reacting to them. This is the ultimate skill of self-awareness and self-management.

While emotions can be very uncomfortable, they cannot hurt you. Let's break down what emotions are: they are simply chemical sensations in our body that are caused by our thinking. There's no emotion that our body cannot handle if we make sure we don't fight against feeling that way. Here's how it works when you experience a challenging emotion during a specific situation: First, you need to allow the initial emotion to flow through your body. Then, when you're ready, become aware of what meaning your mind is adding to the situation. Next, ask yourself if there's a more realistic and balanced way to think about that situation that will create a better outcome for you and your relationships.

Once you understand that your thoughts create your feelings, you can begin to process those feelings to get yourself into a better headspace. Life will open up to you in a big way because you're no longer afraid of facing different situations. You'll know that you're ultimately in control—not of what happens to you, but of how you choose to respond to it.

In my book *The Teen's Guide to Social Skills*, I share a strategy called PAC (Pause, Ask & Challenge), which is a powerful tool to build the habit of managing your emotions rather than just reacting to them.

Pause. When you feel an intense emotion come over you, use that as a cue to pause and take a breath before you react to something. This helps train your brain to pay more attention to your inside world than to your outside one.

Ask. "What am I thinking that makes me feel this way?" This question helps you become aware of your perspective, which will explain your feelings and reactions in the moment.

Challenge. Challenge yourself to find evidence for this thought being true. When you realize your thought is false, it loses its power over you and your emotions, and you're open to taking on a new and more useful perspective.

Let's practice this now. Write down one emotional response you'd like to better manage and then write your answers to each step of this PAC strategy to take back control!

We often believe our feelings are permanent, personal, pervasive, and powerful. These four Ps are actually just myths, and when we believe them, we cause our emotions to become even more intense. Remind yourself instead of the four Ts, the truths about our emotions:

1. **Temporary.** Feelings are caused by the story we're creating in our minds about a situation, but that story is something we can change in the big picture. You're not going to be stuck feeling that way forever.
2. **Tolerable.** Emotions like panic and anxiety are uncomfortable, but you can tolerate them. Part of that is accepting that they're not unbearable. This will help you get through the sensations they're causing.
3. **Totally Normal.** Feeling anxious, worried, or stressed is not unique to you, and it's not a sign that something's gone wrong in your life. Allow space for your feelings to come and go as your thoughts do the same, reminding yourself it's all a normal part of the human experience.
4. **Thoughts.** All thoughts are just thoughts. Simply remind yourself that the sentences in your mind are causing your feelings.

Take a deep breath in, and as you breathe out allow the emotion to flow through your body as you remind yourself of these four Ts.

Expressing to others how we're thinking and feeling is a healthy part of any relationship, but there are helpful (and less helpful) ways to go about this. We want to ensure we don't put others on the defensive and cause an argument by blaming them for why we're thinking or feeling a certain way.

Taking responsibility for your emotions and making it clear that you're not saying your thoughts are the truth is far more likely to put the other person at ease. They will be more open-minded and willing to have a calm and productive conversation with you, rather than wanting to attack back because they're feeling accused of something they didn't necessarily think or do.

Every time you hear yourself say, "You're making me feel (whatever the feeling is)," use that as a cue to correct yourself and say, "Truthfully, I'm feeling _____ because I'm making (their action) mean (your thought about it)."

This may take some practice. But once you begin to experience the reward of more meaningful and calm conversations, you'll realize why this is a habit worth practicing. It will improve all of the relationships in your life!

Reading People

Nonverbal cues are forms of communication beyond spoken words. These cues provide important clues about how someone is really thinking and feeling. Below I break down the three nonverbal cues we typically use to read people during conversations: tone of voice, facial expressions, and body language.

TONE OF VOICE

To improve your ability to connect with others, it's important to practice paying attention not only to what people are saying but also to how they are saying it. This will help you respond appropriately and not miss people's true feelings, especially when it comes to being there to support someone. Take the example of your friend meekly mumbling, "I'm fine." By listening to their tone of voice, you'll know when there's a good chance they're not really fine. Then you might decide it would be good to ask if they need any help with anything, rather than just leaving them to struggle on their own.

FACIAL EXPRESSIONS

So much emotion and meaning is displayed in our facial expressions. Not noticing or misinterpreting them can lead to potential conflict or misunderstandings. For example, perhaps your grandma is clearly showing she's upset with a wrinkled brow and frown on her face, yet you continue to tell a joke she finds offensive. Being able to accurately read others' expressions is a must-have skill if you want to build more connection in your relationships.

BODY LANGUAGE

Body language is a way of communicating without words by using your posture, gestures, and eye contact to express your thoughts and feelings. Typically, if you feel awkward in social situations, you may do things like fidget with your hands, scroll through your phone, pick at your clothes, touch your face, have your head down, or stare away with little to no eye contact with others. This kind of body language can be distracting and feel negative to people when they're trying to talk to you. By paying attention to yourself, you can learn how to display body language appropriate to the situation and the kind of person you want to be, even if you're not necessarily feeling that way in that moment.

Developing our ability to be mindful of our own body language and accurately read others' is a key skill to being able to connect and communicate with others in all social situations.

If you're feeling nervous while speaking to someone, it's easy to want to avoid eye contact and look at something else. However, this can make the other person feel uncomfortable and think that you're not paying any attention to them. So, let's make a new mini habit of improving our ability to look people in the eye when they're talking to us. Typically, you want to maintain eye contact for three to four seconds, then briefly look away before resuming eye contact again.

When you're brushing your teeth each morning (the cue), practice looking yourself in the eye and holding contact for three seconds before looking away and then making eye contact again (the behavior). This is a safe and simple way you can begin to feel more confident holding eye contact (the reward). Once you get the hang of doing it in the mirror, begin to practice holding eye contact with someone you feel comfortable with.

It's tempting to want to shove our hands in our pockets when in conversation with someone if we're feeling awkward or not sure what to do with our hands. The trouble is, this not only looks unconfident, it may also appear suspicious. We definitely don't want to accidentally make someone think we're not trustworthy or open to what they're saying. So here's a new mini habit to practice.

Every time you notice your hands are in your pocket when you're speaking to someone (the cue), remind yourself of "in the box." By this I mean keep your hands out in the open and use gesture movements between the top of your chest and your waist (the behavior). Communication experts consider this to be the most appropriate size and space for hand gestures to display confidence (the reward) without being so big that it's distracting or intimidating for the other person.

We want to get better at managing our own nonverbal cues and also become more skilled at reading others'. Let's start doing this in a familiar place: our own home.

For the next 30 days, whenever you're sitting at dinner with your family (the cue), purposely pay attention to their facial expressions, body language, and tone of voice. Notice how all this changes with their mood. Also notice how even if you couldn't hear what they were saying, you could probably guess the emotion behind it. For example, maybe your brother says he doesn't have a crush on anyone, but his big goofy smile and sly tone of voice say otherwise! Pay attention to how much more engaged you feel in the conversation because you're picking up on how they're really feeling and not just sticking to the surface of what they're saying.

Active Listening

Active listening is an important social skill that involves giving someone our full attention and showing them small signs of engagement throughout the conversation. That's what makes *active* listening active! We're fully involved in the exchange even if we're not the one doing the talking. Listening to others not only helps them feel valued, it also helps them feel better. Research shows that the feel-good chemical serotonin is released in our brain when we feel a sense of belonging and a connection to someone.

Being distracted when someone's talking to you can be the cause of many unnecessary arguments and misunderstandings. Some of the key ways to practice active listening include mirroring, asking questions, and not interrupting.

DON'T INTERRUPT

Interrupting others when they're talking can make them feel disrespected, like you believe what they're saying isn't worth listening to or that what you have to say is more important. This may not be your intention, but it's easy to interpret it that way when you're not giving someone space to express their point of view. Even if you disagree with what they're saying, they still have a right to express it fully and without interruption. A simple way to create healthier relationships is to *interrupt* your urge to interrupt, and listen instead.

ASK QUESTIONS

A quick way to a more meaningful conversation is to ask questions that are relevant to what someone is talking about. Doing this clearly shows them "Hey, I hear what you're saying, and this is what I'd like to know more about."

Some of my coaching students think that asking questions in social situations might make you look unintelligent, especially when asking someone to explain something you don't understand. But it doesn't! It simply shows that you care enough to want to know more so you can properly understand what they're saying. By learning more about others through asking questions, you're continuing to build trust and encouraging them to share more of their thoughts and feelings with you.

MIRRORING

Mirroring is where you reflect words back to the other person to show that their message is being absorbed and understood by you. This isn't about becoming their parrot and echoing every little thing they say. It's more about summarizing the deeper emotion and meaning they're trying to express so they know it's sinking in. It's making statements like, "I understand that you're hurt by what I said last night," or "From what I'm hearing, you feel that it was unfair you weren't given a second chance."

Although we may hear what someone's saying, truly listening and showing them that we understand what they're saying is a skill that takes practice. But it's worth it, because it will help improve every relationship you have!

Even when we're with our best friends, we can get distracted by that notification ding from our phones. Whenever you're having a meal with someone (the cue), leave your phone on silent in the other room—or in your school bag or pocket, if that's appropriate for the setting—and give that person your full attention (the behavior). Notice how much more interesting the conversation seems or how much more you end up talking to the person beside you, simply because your focus is where it needs to be: where you are. Let your brain enjoy serotonin (the reward) for creating more connection with others. This experience shows us that it's worth separating from our phones so we're not separating from who's right there with us!

Responding to others with affirming statements after they take a slight pause in conversation is a really great way to show them that you're actively listening to what they're saying. No one wants to be chatting away and hear silence in return. Affirming is another habit to get into the swing of for better conversations!

Whenever you're having a chat with someone—whether it's your teacher, your mom, your brother, or someone you've just met at a gathering—look them in the eye with the appropriate amount of eye contact. And look for the opportunity to express an affirming statement to let them know you're listening. A simple "Yes, I get what you mean" or even a slight "mm-hmm" while nodding your head can go a long way to showing your interest and helping them feel understood.

A powerful habit to commit to is to interrupt your urge to interrupt. This means every time you feel the urge to blurt out what's on your mind (the cue), choose to pause and redirect your focus back to what the other person is saying and ensure they've completely expressed themselves before you respond (the behavior). You'll see how much this defuses potentially tense situations (the reward).

It can be tough to catch yourself and pause before interrupting, but with practice you will get better at it. Remind yourself how unkind it feels when someone interrupts you, and that can motivate you to commit to the pause! For example, when we're disagreeing with our parents or being disciplined by our coaches, it's easy to get defensive and want to bite back. Don't. Interrupt your urge to interrupt until they've finished expressing themselves to show them the respect they deserve. This will bring more peace and cooperation to all of your relationships.

Empathy

Empathy is about accepting others' emotions without judgment and considering their point of view before you respond. The key is remembering that no matter what we see online or how long we've been friends with someone, we don't really know about the experiences they've been through or how things are going for them that day.

It's easy to fall into thinking that someone's action or response is unreasonable because it's not how you would've acted or felt about things. But this doesn't mean that their way of thinking and feeling is wrong. It's just different. All of us have different upbringings, beliefs, experiences, insecurities, and values. Part of empathy is allowing space for people to feel they way they do, with the understanding that everyone's perspective and emotions are valid.

Although relationships thrive on empathy, we don't have to know someone well to practice empathy. Opportunities for empathy are with us every day, in our friendships, relationships, and interactions with the public. Perhaps you're on a plane near a screaming baby with a flustered mom trying to soothe him. It would be tempting to get angry and stare at the mom with a scowl on your face. But here's where empathy can come into play: ask yourself how you would feel in that situation. Would you want people judging *you*?

The answer is most likely no, right? No one likes to feel ridiculed by others, especially when they're doing the best they can. This is where we have a choice to redirect our perspective to one founded on kindness and compassion. For example, you don't need to be a parent to relate to what it's like to feel overwhelmed by something that's not going your way. By making empathy a priority, you continue the practice of opening your heart to others, even when they're not at their best.

The simplest way to get into the habit of empathy is to simply ask yourself this question: "If that were me . . . ?" Ask this every single time you have the thought to judge or criticize someone for how they're thinking or feeling.

Perhaps your older sister is crying about her boyfriend dumping her. You always thought he was a jerk, and you feel the temptation to tell her to stop crying over him and that she was stupid to date him. Instead, pause and simply ask yourself if you would want someone shaming you for feeling this way. The answer will be no—the last thing a struggling human needs is more judgment. The result is a special bonding moment as you put your arm around her shoulder and let her cry it out. I bet this is exactly what you would've wanted if you were in her shoes.

Let's practice this now. Think about the last time you got frustrated with someone. Pull out your journal or notes on your phone and ask yourself, "If that were me in their situation, how would I want someone to respond?" Write whatever comes to mind. Notice how you, too, would appreciate more empathy and less judgment.

Whenever you feel intense emotions come over you for something someone did, this is your cue to work through them with this journaling exercise. It will help you process the judgmental thoughts that are hijacking your emotions and get you back to a more empathetic place.

1. If I were my most understanding self, what would I think about their actions?
2. If I knew their reaction was triggered by past hurt or a fear that they're not good enough, how would I react differently?
3. What if I choose to love myself and the other person and let us both be humans who struggle sometimes?

One of the best ways to help us practice empathy is to think deliberately about the kind of people we want to be in the world based on our core values and the legacy we want to leave behind. Creating a legacy board and looking at it daily is a powerful reminder to choose empathy in all of your interactions that day.

1. Get a piece of cardboard and markers or pull up a document on your computer. In the center of it, write "I want to be known as the person who . . ." and complete the sentence with whatever comes to mind for you.
2. Write down five values that align with the message of your legacy (for example, courage, kindness, or trustworthiness).
3. Keep this poster somewhere visible and make a habit of looking it over before you head to school each day. This will remind your brain of the core values you'll use to shape your actions today and why it's worth making that choice. In 50 years, you'll be proud of the choices you made and continue to make!

Takeaways

- Being able to better communicate and connect with others involves developing a variety of social skills including confidence, active listening, emotional awareness, body language, and empathy.
- Confidence comes from believing in your own value and embracing a growth mindset.
- Emotional awareness is a skill that can help us manage our reaction to other people.
- Body language and active listening are important ways to show someone that we care and help us respond appropriately to what they're saying.
- Empathy is at the core of human connection and is about accepting and understanding others' feelings and perspective.

Chapter Four

TIME MANAGEMENT

We're told that of all the resources in the world, time is our most valuable; it's also the one that's easiest to waste away if we're not mindful. Procrastinating, running late, forgetting things, and feeling overwhelmed by how much there is to get done are all signs that you can use some help with time management. That's what this chapter is all about. We'll look at simple habits you can use to feel calmer and more in control of your daily life, no matter how many things may be on your to-do list!

Create a Morning Routine

Many of us are in the habit of rolling over and hitting "snooze" on the alarm five times until we're frantically running around the house trying to find our other sock in time for school. This can leave us feeling frustrated and frazzled. We may forget important things at home, which then adds more complications to the day.

Learning how to set up a morning routine that puts you in a good headspace and sets you up for a productive day is one of the best gifts you can give yourself. In fact, research has found that having a routine to start your day can help you feel more in control and reduce your levels of a stress hormone called epinephrine. Although it can take a little effort to get started, it's totally worth it, especially as your commitments continue to grow—school assignments, training sessions, tutoring, and volunteer hours, not to mention chores around the home and spending time with friends. Your schedule isn't going to get any lighter, so now is the perfect time to learn how to take better control of it, starting with a strong morning routine! So, what does that look like?

Typically, most morning routines will involve:

- Waking up at a regular time each day to support your body's internal clock and sleep patterns.
- Allotting about 30 minutes for you to get ready without scrambling around frantically.
- Ensuring you've brushed your teeth and fixed your hair in the mirror.
- Making an effort to do any chores your parents may have asked you to do.

Saying goodbye: It sounds simple, but it's always nice to let your parents or whoever may be home know that you're leaving. A hug goes along nicely, too!

Many of these behaviors are best supported by a strong nighttime routine, which we'll explore together shortly. But for now, let's dive into three specific habits you can practice to create a morning routine that starts your day off right!

UN-ZOMBIFY YOURSELF

It's not unusual to wake up feeling pretty groggy, especially when waking up to an alarm. One simple habit to get into is to go to the bathroom and splash cold water over your face as soon as you wake up. This helps get the circulation going in your face, so it's kind of impossible to stay in zombie-zone once your skin feels the rush of cold water. I do this every single morning to properly wake myself up, and it helps every time!

JUST BEYOND REACH

Given that it's tempting to press snooze on our alarm over and over, the simple solution to this is to get into the habit of putting your alarm out of arm's reach—perhaps on the floor in the middle of your room or on your desk, somewhere where you have to physically get up and turn it off. The discomfort of that noise compels you to get up out of bed to turn it off, and just like that, your day has officially started, likely 30 minutes earlier than if you'd been able to switch off the alarm in the comfort of your own bed.

There's still about an hour before lunch, but you're just about ready to eat your own arm. Sound familiar? When we're in this state, it's hard to concentrate on anything else, and we're quick to snap at others for the simplest of things. So how do we avoid turning ourselves into the hangry monster? Eat breakfast! It really is an important part of fueling you for a successful day ahead.

Aim for foods that are high in protein and carbs to sustain your energy right through until lunchtime. I know the typical excuse is "I don't have time for breakfast." There are two solutions: set your alarm clock 10 minutes earlier, or choose foods you can eat on the run, like toast or a nutritious health bar.

Managing Stress

Whether it's the mounting number of school assignments or the pressure to live up to what you see on social media or your parents' expectation for you to get all As, it's easy to feel overwhelmed as a teen. You're dealing with a lot, and it's perfectly normal to feel stressed out sometimes.

Some level of stress isn't bad. In fact, it's a physiological response that can drive our mind to focus and our body into action. Unfortunately, too many teens feel so much stress that it can begin to harm their happiness and self-esteem if they don't have healthy coping mechanisms in place. Struggling to sleep, regular headaches, nausea, trouble focusing, or the inability to handle your day-to-day emotions are all signs that you need to put some stress-relief habits into place.

The following habits are my favorite ones to help clear my mind and feel less stressed when life begins to feel like a little too much.

Whenever you feel like stress is taking over, your chest is tightening up, and your mind is racing, you've engaged what scientists call the "sympathetic nervous system." This is the system that signals to the body that you're in danger and need to get ready for "fight or flight." To counteract this stress, we need to re-engage the "parasympathetic nervous system." This is the system that can settle our mind down and bring it back to a calmer state.

Simply close your eyes and breathe to a count of three, allowing the air to fill up your lungs right down to your belly. Hold this breath for one second and then breathe out for a count of four. Repeat this for a total of five times, preferably in a quiet space where you can fully focus on your breathing. This slow breathing signals to your body that it is safe and there's no real danger present. You can take a moment to practice this right now, while you're not feeling stressed.

A big reason for excessive anxiety is our need for everything to be perfect. I know it may sound motivational to strive to be perfect, but it's hard to keep this up. The quest for perfection can feel like a lot of pressure.

What's perfect is subjective, so chasing perfection is like chasing unicorns—it's a useless pursuit of something that simply doesn't exist. Perfectionism also slows you down and steals your creativity and productivity, which in turn increases your stress levels.

Whether it's trying to find the perfect meme to text a friend or continually fussing with your drawing in art class because you fear it's not good enough, remind yourself that there's no such thing as perfect. There is only ever giving your best; that is always good enough. By allowing yourself to be human and accept less than A+, you're actually more likely to improve your grades and outcomes because your actions are driven by inspiration and creativity rather than by fear and insecurity. So think of an area of your life where you feel pressure to be perfect and say to yourself, "There's no such thing as perfect. Even if I fall short, I'm proud of myself for giving my best—that's what truly helps me progress toward success!"

So many of us get overwhelmed by life because we don't make time to do the things we enjoy, and instead just do what's expected of us. This activity is about getting into the habit of doing something at least once a week that's purely for your enjoyment.

Grab your notebook, or open a doc on your computer, and write down your answer to these questions:

1. What do you love to do so much that you lose yourself in it whenever you're doing it (that doesn't involve social media)?
2. What's that one thing that always helps you feel better no matter what after you do it? If there's more than one thing that comes to mind, write a few!

Next, looking at what you've written as your retreat for your mind, purposely decide when you're going to integrate it into your weekly schedule. Let your parents know you're doing this and why so they can get on board with supporting you. Your peace of mind will thank you for it.

Learn to Prioritize

Prioritizing ensures you're doing what matters most so you gain traction toward your deadlines and goals. But trying to prioritize tasks in our own head is like trying to memorize an entire grocery list with 25 things on it. Our brains simply aren't made to be able to comprehend and remember all of that at once, which is why it begins to feel like a big fuzzy mess. Instead, the power of prioritizing starts when you write out all the specific things you need to do. These can be included in one overall list for the week, which can then be broken down into a daily list of to-dos.

This exercise in itself is a huge relief for your brain! It no longer has the pressure of trying to hold on to all the tasks. But prioritizing doesn't stop there. It's also about deciding which tasks you're going to complete first and in what order, based on their urgency and importance in relation to your goals.

Taking the time to properly write out, rank, and prioritize your tasks on a daily and weekly basis saves you time in the big picture because you feel way less stressed and more clear-minded about how to tackle your day. This means less procrastinating and more productivity!

To-do tasks can come at you from anywhere and everywhere. So to ensure you're not feeling pulled in a million different directions, create a master to-do list where you write down *everything* you need to get done. This becomes your go-to resource for choosing your daily priorities.

For the next few minutes, brain dump *all* the things that you need to do or remember for the next month—no matter how big or small—onto a piece of paper or the notes section of your phone. Every weeknight, before you shut down your laptop and get ready for bed, look at this list and add anything else that's come up that day that needs to get done. Cross off any tasks you accomplished.

The next habit to build on top of daily updating your master to-do list is prioritizing the top three things you *must* get done that day. You'll determine these based on due dates and importance in relation to your goals. You'll pick three things so it doesn't overwhelm your brain with too many tasks and gives you a clear focus that feels achievable and actionable. This helps you build momentum and feel like you've had a successful day!

New commitments may arise each day that you can't predict, so I believe the best time to write out your Top 3 priorities is as soon as you get home from school. Pull out your master list, add to it any tasks or projects that came up that day, and then on a separate list decide the top three priorities you're going to accomplish that evening. Leave this list somewhere convenient so you'll be able to cross off as you go.

One of the best tips I've been given when it comes to prioritizing and managing my time better is to bite-size my tasks. This helps make things seem less daunting and motivates your brain to get on board with doing them because it's simple and clear what needs to get done.

For example, rather than putting "write history essay" on your Top 3 list, you want to get into the habit of writing a smaller, specific task you're going to do within that bigger project that day, like write the intro or draft the outline.

If you need help breaking down your tasks, start with the end goal in mind (for example, the completed essay) and keep asking, "Okay, so what would I need to know or understand in order to take that step?" Each step becomes a task on your to-do list.

Let's practice this now. Grab your journal or open your to-do list doc, pick one task on your list, and write out the task in three mini steps. See how it doesn't seem quite as daunting to get done when we bite-size the tasks? That's the power of breaking it down!

Scheduling Is Your Friend

If there's one habit that's really going to help you take back control of your life, it's scheduling. I used to resist using a planner or schedule. I thought it would make me feel restricted. But scheduling is in fact how you learn to be more independent and create more of the results you want in your life.

Planning out your schedule engages the purposeful and strategic part of your brain that has your best interests and overall goals in mind. When we try to decide in the moment what we'll do next, we're usually deciding from the lazy part of our brain that just wants to do easy and fun things like watch our favorite show or text our friends. This starts the habit of procrastination! But creating a clear schedule to follow combines a healthy balance of study and work time with leisure and rest time. You're not only far less likely to forget things and run late, you'll also be far more productive and motivated to get things done!

Like an onion, your schedule has different layers. There's the "big picture" monthly schedule that keeps track of significant upcoming events like birthdays or exam week. Then there's the "mid-layer" weekly schedule, keeping track of your weekly commitments and routines. Finally, you have the "core" layer, or your daily schedule, where you get more specific about exactly which tasks you're going to do and when. Now let's dive into specific habits we can use to create a monthly, weekly, and daily schedule!

Did you ever accidentally forget a friend's birthday, miss an appointment with your dentist, or say yes to something happening in two weeks, only to realize you double-booked yourself? That's what happens when we don't keep a "big picture" monthly schedule that clearly lays out what's coming up so we know how to plan and adapt accordingly.

Get yourself a calendar, either one for your wall at home or an app on your phone, and every time you get any sort of future appointment or commitment, put the time and date in your calendar as soon as it's confirmed. If you're using your phone app, you can also set it so your phone will remind you the day before an upcoming event like an appointment or due date.

Choose a time every Sunday to sit down with your calendar and plan your schedule for the week ahead. Then schedule in some personal "me time" (I suggest at least 30 minutes most days of the week) so you don't crowd the calendar and leave yourself without any time to refresh your mind.

Once you have those important things scheduled, it's time to practice a unique scheduling habit called "chunking"—putting together similar tasks—so you stay focused on one activity. This really helps your concentration and productivity levels. Some of the different tasks and activities you can chunk include study time, social time, and family time.

Because most weeks will likely be somewhat similar for you throughout the school year, you can use your weekly schedule as a basic template and adjust it as needed based on upcoming events. For example, 6–8 p.m. can become your study time, 8–9 p.m. your social time to chat with friends and hang on social media, and 9 p.m. your family time before your 10 p.m. bedtime.

My coaching students will sometimes tell me, "I don't know how long to allow in my schedule for my homework because I don't know how long it'll take me to get through these questions." But that's doing it back to front!

If we allow two hours to do our science home-work, it'll take us two hours to get done because every few questions we might pick up our phone or get a snack. Instead, if you tell yourself you only have one hour, you'll likely be more focused because you haven't allowed yourself time to procrastinate so much.

So when it comes to productive scheduling, the question isn't "How long will this take me?" but "How long will I reasonably allow for this task?" Then commit to sticking with the answer to that! You'll be amazed at how much more you'll get through when you decide ahead of time.

Control Distractions

Did you know that it takes your brain 23 minutes and 15 seconds to refocus after it's been distracted from a task? You might think it's not a big deal to spend five minutes procrastinating on your phone. But the real cost comes afterward in the loss of creative and strategic thinking that your brain can't access because it's struggling to get back on track. This is why we need to be more mindful of managing our distractions so we're not falling behind on our schedules.

Technology aside, distractions can also come in the form of other people and other commitments. Perhaps you offered to take on too many tasks, leaving little time for you to have any "me time" or get through your priorities with schoolwork. Wanting to help and contribute as much as you can is a beautiful thing, but you never want to do so at the expense of your own well-being and priorities. You need to allow a reasonable amount of time for yourself first. This isn't selfish; it's self-love. It's important to look after your own needs first, or you'll have nothing to give to others.

Learning how to delegate tasks to someone else, asking for help, and lovingly saying no to things that aren't priorities are important life skills that help you stay focused on things that matter most to you. The next mini habits will help you practice these skills.

The simplest way to keep your brain focused is to keep your phone out of your room during study time. I know your parents have probably nagged you about it, but it really is a powerful way to help you get more done in less time and be able to be your most creative and strategic self!

Research shows that even seeing your phone can mess with your concentration, so the easiest way to power through your schoolwork is to get into the habit of switching off your phone and leaving it in another room before you start studying. Your brain may initially freak out a little if you're used to constantly having your phone with you. But that's okay. It will eventually calm down once you get into the groove with your homework and distract it from its distraction!

To get started with this new habit, think of a place right now where you can put your phone. Write it on a piece of paper you can leave at your desk as a cue to remember to make this a phone-free zone as you sit down for study time!

There are lots of opportunities to be a part of sports teams, social groups, and volunteer causes that help us live a fun and interesting life. But it's good to be mindful of not overloading ourselves because we feel like we have to say yes to everything. Practice the habit of saying "no, thank you" when you're asked to do something or offered to join an activity that's not already in your schedule.

In fact, from a very loving and honest place, you can get into the habit of saying, "Thanks for asking, but I don't have time for that this week. Maybe we can plan ahead for another time soon?" This protects your schedule and commitments but also keeps the offer open so it's not entirely a no—it's just not a yes right now.

One of my main distractions when I was in school resulted from my sister excitedly bursting into my room to tell me something or ask to borrow some clothes. I know she didn't mean to disturb me; she just wasn't aware that I was studying or occupied with something.

One way to control distractions is to get into the habit of letting your friends and family know that you're studying or in the middle of doing something that requires your complete attention. You don't have to do it from a defensive place, just a simple "Hey guys, I'm heading into my room to do (your task) for the next (time duration you've planned). Please don't interrupt me unless it's really important." Just like that, your friends and family are aware of your schedule and less likely to accidentally distract you.

Create a Nighttime Routine

We started this chapter discussing the importance of morning routines, but what really sets you up for a successful morning is an awesome nighttime routine! That's because how tired you feel and how organized you are in the morning largely depend on what you do before you head to bed the night before.

Are your schoolbooks lying all over your floor and your laptop battery on empty? Or have you already packed your school bag for the day and popped your laptop on to charge for the night? It's pretty clear that the latter is going to make for an easier morning. You won't have to run around and gather up your things, because they're already prepped and ready to go!

Then comes the issue of trying to wind our minds down and get ourselves ready for sleep, which is pretty challenging if we're spending the last couple of hours constantly stimulated by the buzzing of our phones or the bright light of our TV and computer screens.

We're going to explore how to handle all this in an upcoming section on sleep habits, but for now we're going to focus on simple habits that you can practice each night to get you organized for the morning. This helps make for a better night's sleep because you're not anxiously worrying you'll forget something.

PACK YOUR BAG

Before you brush your teeth at night, get into the habit of packing your bag with everything you need for the next day, whether it's schoolbooks, your laptop, chargers, sports clothes, your wallet, or anything else you may need. While you're doing this, check if your electronics are charged up. If they're not, place them on chargers right next to your bag so you remember to take them in the morning. Knowing everything is already prepped for you will make for a much easier morning routine.

CHOOSE YOUR CLOTHES

After you've prepped your bag and electronics, use that as a trigger for the habit of choosing your outfit for the next day. Be sure to check the weather forecast so you pick clothes that will be comfortable. Deciding on your outfit the night before and laying it out over a chair or some-where you can quickly grab it in the morning are two huge time-savers. We've all had that expe-rience of racing around trying to find a jacket or realizing the top we wanted to wear is actually stained, so we end up running late. Save yourself that hassle in the morning by getting your outfit ready the night before!

I'm assuming that you're already in the habit of brushing your teeth each night (if not, definitely add that to the list—taking care of our pearly whites is important!), so once you walk back into your room afterward, use that as your cue to set your alarm for the morning. You may think that the light coming through your window will wake you up in time or your parents will come knocking on your door, but it's not up to anyone else but you to ensure you're up in time. Setting an alarm is the most reliable way to do that. If you sleep with your phone out of your room, get yourself a cheap alarm radio or clock that you can use. Remember to put your alarm just out of reach so it compels you to get out of bed as soon as it goes off.

Takeaways

A successful day starts with a successful morning routine, which includes habits like washing your face and eating a healthy breakfast.

Experiencing stress sometimes is normal, and we can learn how to manage it through healthy habits like deep breathing and letting go of perfectionism.

A simple way to stay on top of your tasks and commitments is to create monthly, weekly, and daily schedules that help you structure your days and maximize productivity!

Sometimes there are so many things to get done that you may forget things and miss deadlines. A simple solution to this is to prioritize the top three things you need to focus on first with your daily schedule.

A strong nighttime routine focuses on organizing yourself for the next day through habits like packing your bag and setting your alarm to wake you right on time.

Chapter Five

PERSONAL HEALTH

When we say the word "health," we typically think of eating well and exercising often, but that's just one slice of it. As humans, our mental, emotional, and spiritual health are every bit as important for our well-being. In this chapter, we dive into every aspect of health, so you can learn habits that can help you feel better from the inside out.

Sleep Habits

If I said I could find a way to improve your grades, help you make better decisions, be more creative, feel less stressed, be a safer driver, and memorize new skills—like new dance moves, golf swings, or guitar chords—a whole lot faster, would you be on board? Because that's exactly what establishing awesome sleep habits can do for you!

I know it seems like our brain is just snoozing when we're asleep, but in fact it's incredibly active. It's doing critical things for our mind and body to stay healthy, like repairing muscle cells, recharging energy, clearing out toxins, and storing what you learned that day in your long-term memory. That's why staying up late to cram before an exam doesn't work. You're not giving your mind a chance to fully absorb the info, so it's in one ear and out the other.

Sleep deprivation can also cause chaos in our emotional life as it typically makes us moodier and more reactive to things. Lack of sleep can even lead us to make more impulsive and risky decisions because we haven't given our prefrontal cortex (the part of your brain that controls self-regulation) a chance to recuperate overnight. This means we're more likely to make decisions we'll regret later.

Sleep is just like water and food: we need to get enough of it to help us survive and thrive in life! Yet surveys show that 91 percent of American teenagers get less than the needed minimum of nine hours of sleep each night. If you're one of them, don't beat yourself up. With the overstimulation of social media, school stress, friendship dramas, parental pressure, chores, and commitments, it can be hard to quiet our minds down to settle into sleep. But thankfully, creating healthy sleep habits can make it much easier to get you a whole lot closer to the recommended nine hours of Zs, which will allow you to make the most of every day!

It's good to get into a sleep-time routine at the same time every night to teach your internal clock when it's time to drift off to sleep. To help you stick to this, practice what I call the "4 Ss."

1. **Switch off digital devices.** The blue light from digital screens actually releases chemicals in the brain that signal it's still daytime. So turn off the screen for all electronics one hour before bedtime.
2. **Set up your room.** The best night's sleep is in a cool, dark, and quiet room. The next step is to draw your curtains, switch off any bright lights, and leave on only a dim reading light. Because overheating is a common cause of restless sleep, set your thermostat between 60 and 67 degrees. This will help you feel comfortable throughout the night.
3. **Self-care.** Take a moment to brush your teeth and wash your face, or have a warm shower or bath to wash away the day and help relax your body.
4. **Soothing activity.** Once you've done steps 1 through 3, do about 30 minutes of something soothing for your mind, like reading a novel, solving a crossword, coloring, listening to a podcast or relaxing music, or petting your pet.

BEDS ARE FOR SLEEPING

This habit is about training your mind to connect your bed with sleep . . . and only sleep. This means committing to not doing any other activities, like playing video games, doing homework, checking your phone, or watching TV from bed at any other time during the night. By using your bed for sleeping only, crawling into it at night becomes a trigger for your brain to know it's snooze time.

Jot this down in your journal or on a piece of paper: "My bed is for sleeping only!" By writing this commitment out on paper, you're more likely to remember to stick to it!

RISE TIME

We've spoken about a consistent bedtime, but keeping a regular wake-up time is every bit as important for your sleep health. Waking up at 6 a.m. on a weekday and 11 a.m. on a weekend is going to throw your body clock out of whack big time. Instead, you want to get into the habit of waking no later than two hours later on a weekend than you do on a weekday. So, a 6 a.m. rise time on school days means an 8 a.m. rise time on Saturday and Sunday. Set an alarm on the weekend for two hours later if you need to. It may seem annoying, but it's how you can ensure every night of sleep is restful.

Feeding Your Body

What you eat can affect your mind as much as your body. There's a phenomenon known as the "sugar high," which is the spurt of energy you feel after eating sugary foods like chocolate and cookies. Then the "sugar crash" follows when your body's blood sugar levels plummet, and you're left struggling to keep your eyes open during class after lunch. That's just one example of how consuming too much processed food or junk food can affect your concentration.

Overall, poor food choices can have a domino effect on your daily life. On top of that, research has actually found links between a diet high in sugar and depression, and between an overconsumption of sugar and an increase in anxiety symptoms. Your mind will thank you for being more mindful of what you eat.

A healthy diet is typically a balance of these three main macronutrients: carbohydrates, fats, and protein. Carbohydrates are your main source of energy, protein is what helps grow and repair your muscle cells, and fats maintain a healthy brain function and immune system. When you're consuming too much or too little of these nutrients, your body will struggle with symptoms like sluggishness, weight gain or loss, irritability, skin breakouts, getting sick, digestive issues, and lack of energy to perform at your best during big games or exams!

Part of growing up is beginning to prioritize eating in a way that also feels good in the long term for your mind and body. Now, I'm not saying you shouldn't ever enjoy a sweet treat or indulgent delight. What we're looking for is more of a balance of fueling your body with fresh foods rather than food that comes from a packet or fast-food chain. Plus, eating consistently every few hours throughout the day (starting with breakfast) ensures your body has the energy it needs to perform at its best.

Most people resist the idea of taking things out of their diet. They feel like they're missing out. I prefer to think of it as adding good foods to my diet, so it feels more exciting and like I'm expanding my food choices rather than limiting them.

There are 2,000 types of fruit and over 1,000 veggies, and I bet you haven't come close to trying them all! The habit of adding at least one veggie and one fruit to every meal you eat each day will help ensure you're meeting your daily need for nutrients. Use this habit as a fun experiment and try out all different types of veggies and fruit to see what tickles your taste buds. You'll discover new healthy foods you'll want to include in your daily diet.

Our brains are wired to seek the dopamine hit of sugary, calorie-loaded food. So if we decide in the moment, then we're always going to have the urge to eat that treat. Instead of randomly eating your favorite treats whenever you feel like it, you want to get into the habit of consciously deciding each Sunday night when you're going to eat that special treat once a week.

Then, rather than give into those "must eat this now" urges every time, you can respond to them with a reminder that your favorite food *is* coming. It's just going to be at a specific time, whether it's part of Tuesday night's dinner or Sunday afternoon's snack. This helps prevent the overeating that can sometimes bring that bloated, sickly feeling from eating too much junk too often. So let's decide now. When will you have your treat this week? Commit to that and let the urges be there in the meantime—your treat is coming according to the schedule you set.

Did you know that consuming enough water is every bit as important to your mental health as to your physical health? Considering that 75 percent of your brain is made up of water, as little as 2 percent dehydration can negatively impact its ability to function well. In fact, research has also found links between dehydration and issues like depression and anxiety.

Surveys show a quarter of American kids aged 6 to 19 don't drink water as part of their daily fluid intake. Instead, they're opting for juices, sodas, and energy drinks filled with more sugar than they need. So, the habit to get into is to ensure you stay hydrated throughout the day by getting yourself a reusable water bottle that you keep filled and sip from regularly to reach your needed two to three quarts a day (approximately four refills of a typical 16-ounce water bottle).

Staying Active

The word *exercise* often makes us cringe because it's so much easier to just curl up on the couch and scroll through social media than it is to get up off our butts and get moving. In fact, our brains are wired to want to exert as little energy as possible. Back in the caveman days, it was helpful to conserve energy. We all have a "sloth" in our minds that tries to convince us to just be lazy. Unfortunately we seem to be letting our inner sloth win a little too often. Research shows that teenagers today are as sedentary as 60-year-olds, with 75 percent of teen girls and 50 percent of teen boys not reaching the recommended one hour of sweat-worthy exercise each day.

It's important we make the effort to get into the habit of regular exercise; otherwise, little by little, we'll begin to cause issues for our health. You may notice things like feeling out of breath after climbing up a set of stairs, falling behind the team in practice, or not being able to walk your dog as far as you used to. In the long term, this extra demand on your cardiovascular system (aka your heart) can really take a toll on your well-being. As you get older, it can lead to things like heart disease, type 2 diabetes, high cholesterol, and obesity.

While physical activity can cause temporary physical discomfort, it's a small price to pay for the kick-butt feeling you get afterward. You'll not only feel a boost in self-esteem and body positivity from the body's release of endorphins (the body's "happy chemicals"), but you'll also lower your stress chemicals and increase the ones that help improve your mood. Exercise is a powerful way to ward off mental health conditions like depression and anxiety, and it helps turn around any bad day. Let's give ourselves the gift of that feeling and the physical benefits that come with it more often by starting with these next mini habits!

Our sloth voice is very loud when we try to get it motivated to do something physically challenging for an extended period of time. I like to tell it that we only have to get moving for five minutes, and then if we still don't feel like exercising, we can quit. To help overcome the struggle of getting ready to exercise, get into the habit of telling yourself, "Just five minutes."

The hardest part about an exercise routine is getting started. Often, once you've gotten dressed, put your shoes on, and started moving, you'll actually get the momentum you need to do the full sweat session! And even if you don't, five minutes of exercise is better than none. You're taking action to build the identity of being an "exerciser," which is important in helping you follow through on your daily commitment to get moving! So grab your phone and set a reminder for when you're going to do your five minutes of exercise today. I promise you it's worth it!

We're mindful of sticking to commitments we make with our friends because we care about our friends so much. That's why having a workout buddy is so powerful in helping us show up when it's time for exercise. They keep us accountable and add that extra layer of motivation!

Research has found that having an accountability partner increases your odds of following through on your workout by 65 percent because everything is better when you're sharing it with a friend! So reach out to one of your friends and ask them to become your workout buddy. Together, choose a workout you want to do together daily. Even if you can't meet each other at the same time and place every day, get into the habit of texting each other every afternoon at a specific time to check in on whether you followed through on your workout that day. Think of someone you'd like to be your accountability buddy and make a plan with them now.

Skipping our workouts and sitting on our backsides all day typically leads to the discomfort of feeling sluggish, and your future self suffers because of that. In contrast, following through on physical activity makes your future self feel awesome, with the feel-good chemicals that flood our mind and bodies! So, when the sloth voice tries to convince you it's not worth the effort of working out, speak back to that voice by saying, "This is a gift to my future self that I will be proud of!" If the sloth voice still whines back at you (which it sometimes will do), bring the sloth with you and let it complain its way through your workout if needed. By the end of it, you'll have well and truly reminded it why it's always a win to get moving!

Spiritual Growth

Spiritual growth isn't necessarily linked to being religious. Instead, it's about understanding that there's a deeper part of you, a soul or a spirit that lives within you that needs to be nourished as much as your mind and body.

I'm sure you can think of a time when you've felt deeply stirred by something—whether in the middle of a prayer or while watching a sunrise in awe—and you realized that there is so much more to this universe than what we see with our eyes. I truly felt this when my sister died, and my soul ached deeply at her loss. Yet at the same time I feel empowered by her presence, as if her spirit now lives on within me. Perhaps you've also lost a loved one and can relate to this sense of connection.

Spirituality is about paying attention to your innermost feelings, values, and desires so you follow your true calling in life and allow yourself to be the "you" you were made to be, not the one we sometimes feel pressured to be. I call this connecting to our "inner compass." Practicing spirituality in your life is worth it because of the deep sense of fulfillment and meaning it can bring. In fact, research has found that the more spiritual you are, the more resilient you are in facing difficulties, and the greater overall quality of life you have. This is because lack of spirituality can leave you with the idea that your struggles are in vain and without purpose, which often leads to bitterness and suffering.

There are a variety of ways you can bring more spirituality into your life, including journaling, praying, meditating, practicing yoga, singing, painting, lighting candles, and reflecting with nature. There's no right or wrong way to practice being spiritual. There's simply the way that brings you peace and helps slow your mind down so you can pay attention to your inner compass and connect to a source deeper than yourself.

Practicing gratitude is one of the most powerful ways to grow your inner peace and spirituality. Research has found that practicing gratitude releases feel-good chemicals in our brain that put us in a better mood and widen our perspective so we're able to see more of the big picture and feel more optimistic and hopeful.

To ensure that gratitude becomes a daily practice in your life, set up the habit of writing down three things you're grateful for each morning before you eat your breakfast. Whether it's gratitude for your mom dropping you off at school, the food you're getting to eat, or your friend who asked you out on the weekend, there's always something to be grateful for. Writing three things down before breakfast each day will train your brain to remember this so your spirit will feel strong even when life gets tough.

Meditation is simply a practice of learning how to still your mind and stay present in each moment. You might have heard of meditation before and think it sounds boring, but it's actually incredibly relaxing and something that can help you find peace no matter how overwhelming life may feel.

If you've never meditated before, I encourage you to start small and get into the habit of two minutes of meditation once you get home from school each day. This will help you leave the stress behind and pay attention to soothing your spirit for a moment before diving into your schedule for the evening. Use the action of putting your school bag on your bedroom floor as the cue to get out your headphones. Go to YouTube and search for "two-minute meditation for teens." Select one of the videos and lie down on your floor as you're guided through a simple meditation exercise.

Life can get so busy that we're racing around to our next class or team practice. More often than not, we're staring down with our eyes glued to our phones, leaving us spiritually and emotionally disconnected. This slowly eats away at our spiritual and mental health, because humans crave connection.

This habit is something you can do anywhere and everywhere: simply smile more often at people. Smiling helps lift your mood and the mood of everybody you smile at. When you lift a person's mood, they're more likely to smile at someone else, which lifts that person's mood and makes them want to smile more at someone else, and so on! Realizing the power of something as simple as a smile can help your spirit feel more connected to this world and remind you that your actions do make a difference. So smile more and smile often.

Emotional Regulation

Emotional regulation is not allowing your feelings to dictate your actions. It's similar to emotional awareness, but one step further. You not only recognize what you're feeling, but you also focus on not letting it hijack your reaction.

Now, please don't think I'm saying we should resist or fight against our feelings—that only causes them to build up and erupt in bigger ways. Remember, the human brain is wired for survival. It's quick to react and assess most things as a potential threat and something worth stressing over, so it often causes us more emotions of overwhelm, frustration, and anxiety than it needs to.

That instant thought-feeling trigger is going to happen whether we like it or not. We can't change that automatic part of our brain. What we can do is engage the "purpose" part of our brain to choose the way we respond to our automatic thoughts and feelings. The choice we make will make them either more or less intense.

The tempting choice is to instantly believe and react to our thoughts and emotions, and let them dictate our next action. However, this will often lead to more arguments, more misunderstandings, more procrastination, more second-guessing, more ruminating, and, ultimately, more quitting!

Emotional regulation is about allowing space for the discomfort of the initial feelings that come from your ANTs (page 7) and then purposefully choosing to respond in a way that helps you process that emotion while taking action. You want that action to be driven by your values and goals, not by your temporary feelings, because feelings often lead to actions we later regret. Once you know how to regulate your emotions, you gain so much power over the actions you take on a daily basis, consistently getting you closer to your goals!

GET OUT OF YOUR MIND
AND INTO YOUR BODY

The next time your ANTs (page 7) trigger an intense emotion, rather than reacting to or resisting it, practice these five steps:

1. **Pause.** When you notice an intense emotion come over you, pause.
2. **Name.** Name the emotion. ("I am feeling ____.")
3. **Locate.** Where in your body can you feel this emotion?
4. **Describe.** What sensations is it causing? Is it fast or slow, hot or cold, a sticky or a slimy feeling?
5. **Feel.** Taking deep breaths, allow the feeling to flow through your body. No matter how uncomfortable it may be, your body can process any emotion if you allow the feeling to naturally dissipate without fear or judgment.

Getting into the habit of these five steps will help you slow down your mind, relax your body, and reduce the intensity of your emotions. From there, you'll be able to see more options for how you can choose to respond to and handle the situation.

THE FIVE-YEAR RULE

Scientists have found that negative emotion narrows our mindset. We're unable to see the big picture, making simple setbacks seem bigger than they are and causing us to catastrophize and imagine the worst-case scenario. An easy way to break the habit of that stressful cycle is to ask yourself, "How much will this matter five years from now?"

By stepping back and looking at the situation from a future place far removed from the current moment you're struggling with, you're able to see things in a different way, with a more balanced perspective. So think of something that's been overwhelming you lately and jot down your answer to this question: "How will I think about this in five years?" For example, will you still be worried that you failed that algebra exam or that your crush didn't reply to your text? As someone who's a few years ahead of you, I promise you that you will barely even remember it happened at all!

When you're struggling emotionally, get into the habit of reaching out and speaking to someone about how you're feeling. This could be your parents or guardians, a friend, your sibling, a coach, a counselor, a psychologist, or another trusted adult. Please never try to get through it all on your own.

You may feel resistant to reaching out to someone because you fear being judged or think they won't understand. But remember that everyone is human, and so we all face a full range of emotions as we find our way through the highs and lows of life. Sharing our feelings with someone else who has an outside perspective can help us find fresh insight or give us advice or validation to feel that little bit better again.

It's best to decide who we can reach out to ahead of time, so in your journal or notes on your phone, complete this sentence: "The next time I'm feeling really overwhelmed, I will reach out to . . ." List two or three people you feel comfortable turning to for support.

Takeaways

- Getting enough sleep is one of the most important ways to recharge your mind and body. Aim for at least nine hours each night by setting up a bedtime routine.
- Healthy eating isn't about depriving yourself; it's about adding in more wholesome foods that have a good balance of protein, carbohydrates, and fats to support your energy throughout the day.
- Motivate yourself to get moving more often using habits that help silence the sloth voice and gain momentum with exercising.
- Nourishing your spirituality is about connecting with something beyond yourself through activities like journaling, meditating, practicing gratitude, and making an effort to smile more often at people to share those good vibes.
- Emotional regulation is learning how to better manage your thoughts and emotions through practicing habits like reaching out for help when you need it.

Chapter Six

FOSTERING RELATIONSHIPS

Like flowers, relationships require care and attention to grow and bloom. It's easier to care for some relationships than others. For example, it's typically easier as a teen to get along with our friends than our parents or teachers. However, all relationships play an important part in helping us navigate our way through adolescence. We want to ensure we're looking after them all (even when we don't feel like it). Though fostering relationships takes effort, by the end of this chapter you'll understand why the reward is worth the effort.

Communication

Unhelpful communication habits can make it challenging to develop fun and meaningful relationships. When we push away our own wants, needs, and desires to try to make someone else happy, we're doing what I call "people pleasing." Of course it's a positive thing to be mindful of other people's needs, but the issue comes when we're doing it at our own expense and not valuing ourselves enough to express our own opinions. This is crippling to your self-esteem because you're not allowing yourself to be the true you.

We don't want to go to the other extreme of communicating with aggressiveness by always saying what we think and feel without considering others. This naturally leads to conflicts and arguments. People may end up resenting us or distancing themselves from us because they don't feel valued in our presence. The healthy balance to help all relationships thrive is called *assertiveness*. This means expressing your thoughts and feelings honestly while still showing respect for another person's perspective.

One of the most meaningful parts about having friends and family is getting to be there for each other when times get tough and we're feeling down in the dumps. Sharing those moments is what helps your relationships become more resilient because you know you can count on each other for support. However, for this to happen, you have to practice getting better at being open and truthful about your innermost thoughts and feelings even when they may feel like a bit of a mess. By doing so, you show the other person that it's safe for them to do the same. That's what truly builds trust and connection in relationships.

Don't let the discomfort of being vulnerable stop you from expressing how you truly think and feel. Instead, use the discomfort as a cue to practice being brave enough to express what's on your mind. To make this a little easier, start getting in the habit of honestly expressing that what you're about to say is hard for you to open up about. For example, "I want to share this with you because you matter to me, but I do feel a little nervous telling you about it, so I'd appreciate your patience as I do my best to put it into words."

Remember, you're speaking with another human who more than likely can relate to the discomfort you're feeling about opening up about something personal. Explaining that you still want to tell them despite your struggle is showing them that your relationship is worth the discomfort. This helps deepen your connection with them. So think of something you've been struggling to open up about and one person with whom you can practice this habit of being brave and expressing yourself—even if your voice shakes.

Most people get asked "How are you doing?" so often that they default to an automatic response of "good," "not bad," or "okay." Now, that's perfectly okay when interacting casually with everyday people in our lives, like a bus driver or a postal carrier, but when it comes to our close friends and family, we want our communication to be meaningful.

A simple habit you can practice is asking, "How are you, *really*?" from a genuinely curious place. That one extra word of "really" will catch people's attention and likely shift them out of default mode. It also shows your extra layer of care, because so many people feel like people ask how they're doing out of habit. You're far more likely to get a thoughtful and honest response that can open up a more meaningful conversation and connection for both of you. Starting tomorrow, commit to practicing this habit on at least five people and notice how often it leads to a meaningful conversation with them.

Expecting people to know what you're thinking without explicitly expressing it is going to set you up for a lot of unnecessary stress and frustration in your relationships. A simple way to begin to create healthier relationships is to practice the habit of EET (express, explain, and thank):

Express. When you realize that you have a specific need or preference you'd like someone to understand, make the effort to calmly and clearly communicate that desire to them.

Explain. Take a brief moment to explain why it matters to you. For example, let your dad know it helps your personal space feel respected when he takes a moment to knock first before entering your room.

Thank. When people take a moment to hear us out about our wants—whether they agree or disagree—thank them for giving you a chance to express and explain yourself.

Think of someone you've been expecting to understand your needs without expressing them and then make a note to practice this EET habit with them by the end of the week!

Conflict Resolution

Given that we all have different preferences and personalities, disagreements and clashes in perspectives will arise in relationships. That's unavoidable. What is avoidable and what you *do* have control over is letting a disagreement escalate into a heated argument filled with yelling, swearing, and accusations that create even more problems for you both. Instead, you can choose to deal with disagreements in a calm and reasonable way that works toward finding a fair resolution for everybody. That's your choice.

Our brains are very quick to react to potential threats and dangers. It's easy for us to immediately jump into attack and blame mode where we want to prove we're right and the other person is wrong. The problem is this often comes at the cost of being a good human and damages relationships. However, the good news is that we can override that default setting in our brain and learn how to handle potential conflict in a way that defuses tense situations and maintains healthy relationships.

Conflict resolution is one of the most important skills you can develop to feel more at peace with your family, build resilient friendships, and navigate school challenges like teachers or coaches you don't connect with well. You don't want to be known as the hothead who can't control their emotions when someone disagrees with you or shares critical feedback. Instead, the goal is to be someone who knows how to constructively disagree with someone and be solution-minded. This is not only how you'll get along better with your teachers, coaches, peers, and colleagues in your future career, it's also how you'll land more opportunities and promotions! Being skillful at handling conflict is one of the best qualities a leader can have.

The first rule to solving conflict is to ensure you do not make it personal by attacking someone's character or their worth. They have equal rights to share their opinion. Just because someone sees something differently from the way you do doesn't make them a bad person. You can disagree with someone without disliking them for their actions or point of view.

Instead of making "you" statements about their character, be focused on taking ownership of your perspective by using "I" statements. For example, rather than saying, "You are a cruel person" or "You are thoughtless," instead say, "I felt hurt when you didn't invite me" or "I am struggling to understand what you were thinking that made you do that." This habit allows you to express your perspective while refraining from placing blame and making sweeping statements about their personal character.

Think of a recent conflict you experienced and an "I" statement you could use going forward. Jot it down!

Conflict can rapidly escalate into a full-blown screaming match if we speak over the other person and don't let them have their say. Often, this happens because we're too focused on trying to prove our point. The simple solution is this: no matter how much you disagree with their opinion, be quiet and listen. Sometimes people want nothing more than to feel like their perspective has been heard before they're able to let it go and move on.

When you're in a tense moment with someone, hit that internal pause button and hear them out. Take deep breaths while you're listening to keep yourself calm and genuinely keep an open ear to what they're saying. We are more likely to appreciate the logic and fairness of their argument and find some sort of resolution if we simply listen—not to judge, but to understand. Take a moment to reflect on someone you often butt heads with. Then, commit to hearing them out the next time you disagree and notice the difference it makes.

APOLOGIZE WHEN YOU'RE NOT
PROUD OF HOW YOU ACTED

The most important thing to do if you ever do or say something that you're not proud of is to not let your ego get in the way. Instead, get into the habit of apologizing by saying something like, "I'm sorry I did that. I can see it wasn't right to do." A genuine apology where you look the person in the eye and say it meaningfully can go a long way to helping them feel respected and forgive you for what happened. Then you can work toward mending the relationship rather than damaging it further.

On the flip side of this, be open to forgiving others for times when they do something out of character. This can sometimes take time, but don't shut down the idea of forgiving someone for making a mistake when you can tell they're genuinely sorry for it. Carrying a grudge against someone only punishes you because you're the one having to carry the weight of it.

Let's pause and jot down answers to these questions:

1. Is there something you've done recently you're not proud of and want to apologize to someone for?
2. Who is the person and when will you apologize?
3. Is there a grudge you're holding against someone you can choose to forgive and move on from?
4. Who is the person and when will you release that burden?

Positive Relationships

As we grow up, it's important to be mindful about the people we choose to surround ourselves with, starting with our friends. I remember trying to hold on to some friendships even when it meant I was doing things I felt uncomfortable with simply because I thought that's what true friends did. But the truth is true friends won't ever ask you to compromise your values or do something that jeopardizes what's important to you.

The goal is to have friends who help bring out the best in you. It's also important to ensure you prioritize friends who are there both for the fun times and the times when you need someone to lean on and confide in. You want to go beyond common interests and look at what you have in common in values and in character so you can help each other grow into people you both feel proud of. This often means extending beyond our friendship groups and peers and reaching out to form strong relationships with our teachers, coaches, and trusted adults we feel connected to.

In fact, seeking out mentors in people we admire is one of the most valuable ways to navigate the turbulence of being a teen. Having a trusted adult who has more life experience than you can help you gain so much more strength and clarity on how to handle tough situations. You may be resistant to reaching out to adults because you're worried they're just going to lecture you. But most mentors are simply trying to be the people they needed when they were younger. They were once struggling teenagers, too.

Keep an open mind to confiding in trusted adults and growing a strong bond with them. Their wisdom and guidance can truly be what puts you on the best path in life. And maybe one day you'll be able to do the same for a future teen.

A good habit to help build strong, positive friend-ships is to pay attention to whether your friends are making decisions and acting in ways that you yourself want to. You don't want to compromise yourself just to fit in. If your friend's behavior doesn't align with who *you* want to be in the world, make an effort to seek out friends whose behavior does! It's not that we have to be mean or push other friends away, but we do want to ensure we're prioritizing people who help us live true to the values of honesty, kindness, and respect.

How do we find those friends? By *being* that friend! Be the friend who is thoughtful and gen-erous but also knows how to have your own back. You will attract friends who have the qualities you believe in. Briefly take a moment to write down the top three qualities you value most in a friend and one or more of your friends who have those qualities.

Having a positive role model and mentor to bounce your thoughts off of and receive advice from is invaluable. If you don't have a mentor already, brainstorm a list of adults in your life you trust, look up to, and feel comfortable talking to (besides your parents). You'll want to consider their experience and what's most relevant to your personal goals (see page 14). Then jot down this list in your journal, phone, or computer.

Reach out and ask if you can schedule some time to talk to them about becoming your mentor. Share your goals and challenges with them. Tell them why you feel they could be really helpful to you. If they're receptive (which they most likely will be!), get into the habit of doing a 15- to 30-minute check-in with them—in person or over the phone—every two weeks to receive their feedback and guidance on your goals and struggles.

We're able to listen to and learn from some of the best mentors and role models with a simple tap of our finger! There are thousands of podcasts and online videos filled with amazing advice, tools, and strategies you can practice to become more successful and overcome your challenges.

So, the next time you're due to do your chores, get your headphones, jump on your favorite podcast app, type in a topic or life skill you're interested in learning more about, and pick an episode to listen to. Given that chores don't usually require a lot of your brainpower, you can get stuff done while learning some really valuable life skills! Visit this book's Resources section for some podcasts to help you get started. You can also write to the podcast host and ask questions they can answer on their show, and learn what other resources they recommend for you to get extra support.

Be Social

Your phone buzzes as you get another text from a friend asking you whether you're joining them at the game tonight, and you sigh. You really can't be bothered to get dressed and ask your mom for a lift when you're so warm and cozy scrolling social media from your couch. You go to text your friend that you can't make it and maybe next time . . . But here is where I want you to pause for a quick pep talk!

I know many of you can relate to the above scenario. You may say that you prefer to socialize this way because conversations through texts are easier. You don't have to awkwardly deal with other people you don't know or be worried someone might be judging what you're wearing or how you look. So why bother making the effort in person anymore?

Well, statistics tell us the average American teen spends about nine hours a day on their phone, yet the current generation of teens (Gen Z) reports that they are the loneliest generation on record. Social media can bring plenty of fun and entertainment to our friendships, but we want to ensure we're still making an effort for in-person interactions with our friends. Studies show that teenagers who had close emotional bonds with friends at 15 years old experienced less anxiety and depression and greater self-worth 10 years later compared with teens who didn't prioritize their friends.

The most memorable moments of your teen years will be the moments you experience in real life together with your friends. So, let's think of social media and online communication as a way to stay connected between times when we're socializing in person but not as a replacement for it. The awkwardness you sometimes feel interacting with others in person is a small price to pay for the reward of growing a deep and meaningful friendship with someone where they've got your back no matter what and you've got theirs.

ORGANIZE WEEKLY "TIGER TIME" WITH FRIENDS

Get into the habit of creating memories offline with your friends by committing to spending at least one hour per week with them outside of school. Use Sunday evenings as your cue to call or text your friend to discuss when you're both free to hang out that week. (Put this in your calendar and set a reminder.) Go the extra mile and suggest a fun activity you could enjoy together like going for a hike, shopping at the mall, or having a movie marathon on the weekend.

Make this time with your friend what I call "tiger time," where you guard that time fiercely and don't let anything take it away from you, like a mama tiger protecting her cubs. Protect that time with your friend like it's sacred, because for your mental health and the bond of that friendship, it is!

PICK ONE EVENT A MONTH
TO GO TO AND ENJOY!

From sports games, musicals, and plays, to fund-raisers, themed nights, and guest speakers, there's always an event on the school calendar that gives you the opportunity to practice being social and make memories with your peers and friends. If you're a homeschooler, jump online to research social events being held by local homeschool groups! As tempting as it is to lounge around in your room, get into the habit of picking one school event each month to go to, like watching the basketball game against the local rival or joining in the games night fundraiser for the school, and invite at least one friend to join you! If you feel like you don't have anyone to ask, practice being brave and go anyway, as this is the perfect chance to make some new friends while you're there!

The initial effort of having to get there is usually well worth the fun you have and the things you learn while you're there. Sharing that experience with a friend gives you more things to chat about and another new memory to share.

A habit to stack on top of the previous one is making the effort to speak to at least one new person whenever you're out at a social event. This is a great way to practice your social skills and overcome your shyness when chatting with people. It may mean some temporary discomfort or nervousness, but I've found that most people are friendly and open to having a chat.

Keep your eye out for someone who looks like they're feeling a little left out or could use some company, go up to them, and introduce yourself. If you already know them but not that well, ask a simple open-ended question like, "Hey, what are you enjoying about this so far?" Let the conversation flow from there. That chat may be the spark of a new friendship!

Be Kind

Everyone has a superpower called *kindness* that if used more often would help all of us humans struggle less. No matter how big or small, the gift of kindness can help us find a reason to smile on a tough day and remind us of the good that is ever present in our world. In fact, research has found that students who did daily acts of kindness for six weeks increased their happiness levels by over 40 percent.

The trouble is, kindness can be very easy to take for granted, especially from our parents and teachers. We may feel we're entitled to have these people be nice to us. But we're not owed the right to everyone always being kind. And when we show up from this place of expectation, we tend to act in less than kind ways. As we grow up and gain more independence in the world, we want to be mindful not to do it at the expense of our character. We want to continue making the effort to be kind and respectful to everyone—even adults who can sometimes get on our nerves. Their concerns usually come from a well-intended place. Being our best selves and taking the time to actually listen to them can go a long way toward keeping the relationship healthy and happy for everyone.

You may feel resistant and want to argue that you're not being respectful to people because they're not being respectful to you. But the truth is that your reaction to their actions, like if you yell or swear back at them, is *your choice* and not their fault. Being disrespectful only punishes you and leaves you feeling miserable, adding to the negativity and judgment in the world. If we want less negativity and conflict, it starts with you and I stepping up and setting the example that kindness is *always* possible even when someone isn't being kind or fair themselves. Be the breath of fresh air in someone's day, and be kind always.

One of the simplest ways we can practice kindness daily is to ensure we always hold the door open for the person behind us. It seems such a small act that it's almost insignificant. But it's not small to the person behind you; it's letting them know that you see them and are mindful of looking out for them. In a world where many people battle the idea of feeling invisible and like no one cares, holding the door can be such a powerful gesture that it can turn their day around.

Practice the habit of paying attention when you're opening a door. If you notice there's someone coming up behind you, pause for a moment and hold it so they can walk through, too. Whether it's your brother, your teacher, or a stranger on the street, hold the door open for them and keep them believing in the goodness of people.

CHANGE THE QUESTION ("IF THAT WERE ME . . . ?")

Being kind is challenging when someone is purposely being rude or unpleasant toward us. A powerful habit that helps me show up in the world from a generous place is to first pause and remind myself that cruel behavior most often comes from a place of pain from past hurt or insecurities.

Rather than thinking "How dare they do that?!" break the cycle of negativity by flipping the question to "How would I appreciate being responded to right now if deep down I was just really afraid or hurting?" The answer to that is always compassion and kindness. Giving ourselves the benefit of the doubt by choosing to see the good in us even if we're not acting that way—that's what helps us find our way back to our best selves, and we can do the same for others. Jot down the name of one person you sometimes find challenging to be around and commit to choosing to see the good in them this week—for the sake of both of you!

I know you've probably had these two words drilled into your head since you were a kid, but in our daily lives we too often forget to say thank you. Making others feel appreciated is a beautiful way to bring kindness and love to their day, and there's always more room for that in our world! Whether it's the cafeteria worker passing your lunch to you, your teacher giving you a handout, or your friend staying late to help you study, be sure to always express your gratitude and thank people for their actions.

The key is to say it like you mean it, with a genuine smile while looking them in the eye. Not only does it feel great for us, our "thank you" also makes their day and can be the ripple effect of more kindness in someone else's day! Think of at least one person you're going to be sure to thank tomorrow. Jot down their name.

Takeaways

- Being open and honest in our communication is important to helping relationships grow stronger!
- Using "I" statements and hearing people out are valuable ways to help reduce and resolve conflicts in relationships.
- Although it sometimes takes effort, going out and being social with your friends is worth the time invested in it for the way it deepens your friendships and improves your mental health.
- You cannot overrate the value of being kind, so give others the benefit of the doubt before judging them harshly. Most people are usually well intended.

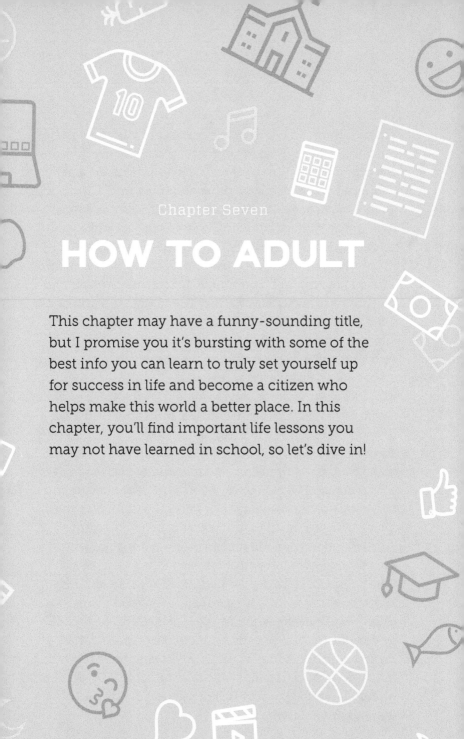

Chapter Seven

HOW TO ADULT

This chapter may have a funny-sounding title, but I promise you it's bursting with some of the best info you can learn to truly set yourself up for success in life and become a citizen who helps make this world a better place. In this chapter, you'll find important life lessons you may not have learned in school, so let's dive in!

Learn to Budget

The day I turned 14 (the age you can start a part-time job in Australia), I began working at a local shoe store every Thursday evening and most weekends. It was sometimes a pain in the butt having to juggle other commitments, like schoolwork, playing sports, and catching up with friends. But when I'd see my paycheck come in, I'd feel a satisfied smile spread across my face, knowing that I'd earned every dollar of it.

Not having to ask your parents for some cash is such a freeing feeling. You really begin to feel independent and more in charge of your own life. The trouble is many of us don't pay much attention to saving money once it's ours. Suddenly that $50 or $500 you had quickly diminishes to zero, and you're back at square one—or worse, you may end up in debt and owe even more!

Thankfully, learning how to budget is how you can avoid constantly ending up broke and help build your path toward financial freedom and independence as an adult. A budget is a simple calculation of your monthly income with your outgoing expenses so you can determine how much you have left to spend on what you *want*. You just have to ensure you're taking care of your essential costs first, like paying for your phone bill or car insurance (if you're old enough to drive).

Sticking to your budget can be hard, but that's why all great budgets start with a clear savings goal in mind. This helps you stick to your budget even when something looks tempting to buy. For example, as a teen I managed to save $20 a week toward my goal of buying a new phone by deciding to bring my own lunch to work rather than buying it from the food court. It might not sound like much, but by doing this, I managed to save an extra $520 over six months, and that paid for half of my new phone and got me there so much faster!

Although your expenses right now might not be huge while you're living at home with your parents, that will quickly change once you graduate from high school (groceries, internet, and phone bill, for example). Now is the perfect time to start taking control of your money through budgeting. It's a skill that will repay you big time in the future—literally! If you start integrating these mini habits into your life now, your 30-year-old self will be high-fiving you for it!

KEEP A SEPARATE SAVINGS ACCOUNT

One of the best budget mini habits I got into as a teen was saving money in a place used exclusively for my long-term goals. By keeping your savings separate from your everyday spending money—whether it's in a piggy bank in your room or an actual account with a bank—you won't accidentally overspend on something else or be tempted to do so!

Stick to that savings commitment by writing down three things you'd love to have in the next two to three years, whether it's a new laptop, your first car, or $5,000 in savings when you head to coding school. Put a star next to the one that's most important to you to remind yourself of its importance. This will help you if the urge to spend beyond your budget creeps in!

How do we know what our budget is and how much to put into savings? On the first day of each month, get into the habit of sitting down with a paper and pen, or opening up a Word doc or spreadsheet, and go through the following steps:

1. Determine your monthly income by adding up the total money you'll receive from *all* sources (your part-time job, weekly allowance, etc.).

2. Calculate your total *essential* expenses for the month. If you're living at home, thankfully most big essential expenses are taken care of by your parents, but many teens have expenses like phone bills, eating out, and public transportation or gas for their car.

3. Determine how much money you have left over by subtracting essential expenses from your income.

4. Split the money left over so that you have 50 percent for your monthly spending money and 50 percent to put in savings toward your goal.

5. Monitor and adjust as necessary. Life is unpredictable and unexpected expenses may occur. Get in the habit of pulling that extra money from your "wants" budget and not your savings—that's always your priority!

SAVE WITH YOUR STUDENT ID

Did you know that some of your favorite brands, including Nike, American Eagle Outfitters, Forever 21, Old Navy, Apple, Best Buy, and Sony, offer discounts to high school students? This is such a fun and simple way to save yourself some money and stick to your budget! Be sure to get into the habit of asking if there's a student discount when you purchase something, whether online or in person. The worst someone can say is no. If you're not yet in high school, stay informed about places that do offer a student discount so that when you become a high schooler, you can supercharge your savings!

Pay It Forward

I remember the first time I heard someone say "Pay it forward." I pictured people standing in a line passing money to the person in front of them. While the definition of paying it forward isn't quite that literal, it is about passing on to someone else something of value you've received from someone. It's all about thinking beyond yourself.

A personal example of this happened while I was waiting in traffic on my way to a school talk, and a man came up to my car window to let me know I had a flat tire. Had he not gone out of his way to do that, I would've blown my tire and missed my presentation completely. I was extremely grateful to him, but I didn't have a chance to say anything more than a quick thank you. When I got home that night, I had an email from someone asking if I could spare 20 minutes to give some advice on how to start their own coaching business. This was a chance for me to pay it forward and give them some of my time to help them out without expecting anything in return. It was a truly wonderful feeling.

I want you to think of a time where you've felt genuinely grateful for someone's thoughtfulness. Perhaps it was a teacher who stayed late to help you with a math problem or a friend who gave up a more exciting Saturday night to talk with you when you were feeling low. These are examples of opportunities to pass that goodness forward by doing a good deed for someone else. Sometimes this value can come in the form of money, like giving your spare change to a homeless person on the street or paying for the smoothie of the person behind you. But typically it's a form of kindness and generosity—like letting a stranger know their wallet has fallen out of their pocket or volunteering at the local animal shelter.

I want to inspire you to make more effort toward prioritizing acts of kindness in your daily life. You know how good it feels when someone does the same for you simply because they can. Kindness for the sake of kindness fills up your heart with a sense of purpose and joy. As humans, we are wired for contribution—something easy to forget in today's society that is all about personal success and accomplishment. As you practice paying it forward, you'll soon realize that true fulfillment in life isn't about what you're achieving but who you are *being* in the world, and that you are putting out into the world what you are grateful to have received.

The simplest way to bring joy through kindness is to get into the habit of intentionally giving a genuine compliment to one person every single day. This could be letting a girl in your grade know you love her sweater, telling your waiter how much you enjoyed their service, or thanking your bus driver for always being friendly and on time. Too often we let these kind thoughts stay in our own minds, yet if spoken aloud they have the power to make someone else smile and boost their self-confidence!

Your goal for tomorrow (and every other day after!) is to compliment at least one person on something you like or admire about them. There's always something to appreciate about everyone. Look and you'll see!

Our society is much like a competitive, self-defeating race in which many of us are scurrying around and barging ahead of one another. It's the complete opposite of community and care, so let's be the change instead and get into the habit of giving way.

Whenever you're in a public place where there's limited seating (your cue!), like public transport or waiting on a park bench, and you see there's someone standing next to you, get into the habit of offering up your seat for them to take. Sure, you may lose your comfortable spot, but you gain the satisfaction of knowing you're being a kind person. You have no idea what's happening in that person's day, but no matter what, you've helped make it that little bit easier, and that's something you should always feel proud of! Try this the very next time you have the opportunity.

Get into the habit of volunteering for or donating to a local cause to give back to your community. Set a reminder on your phone for the 8th of every month so you don't forget to do it! There's an endless list of what you can do to get involved in charitable causes, including (but certainly not limited to):

- Volunteering at local community centers like nursing homes and animal shelters
- Donating the clothes you've outgrown to a local thrift store
- Signing up for a fun run to raise money for a charity
- Making a donation to a cause you hold close to your heart
- Joining the local environmental team to help clean up your local parks and community areas
- Donating food to a food pantry or serving meals to those in need
- Drawing artwork to send to troops overseas or to senior citizen homes

Think Green

Let's play a game! Guess which of the following statements is/are true:

a. There are approximately three trillion trees in the world, which is about half the number there were back before humans started practicing agriculture 12,000 years ago.
b. The average American creates an average of 4.5 pounds' worth of trash each day.
c. About 75 percent of America's waste is recyclable, but we only recycle around 30 percent of it.

Believe it or not, *all* of the above are actually true, and that's why being mindful of making environmentally friendly choices is an important part of learning how to adult. From what we package our food in to how long we leave our lights on, our daily choices have an impact on our environment because of the pollution they create.

The good news is that we can all do our part as responsible citizens to reduce that waste and minimize the impact each of us has on this incredible world we're so lucky to call home. Recycling is one of the simplest yet most impactful ways we can do this, as recycling even one plastic bottle saves enough energy to run a 100-watt bulb for four hours! You're reducing not only the waste in landfills but also the waste sent out into the atmosphere. It's a win-win!

As you can see, caring for our world doesn't mean we have to radically change our whole lifestyle. We simply need to make an effort to be more mindful of making eco-friendly choices, and we can start by putting these next mini habits into action!

Whenever you go to throw something out in the trash, whether it's a soda bottle or used printer paper, pause for a moment and ask yourself, "Is this recyclable?" The majority of items we use on a daily basis—paper, plastic, cardboard, aluminum cans, and glass—are recyclable, but we're often too distracted when we're throwing things out to even notice.

So, get into the habit of using the trash can as a cue to ask yourself if your rubbish is better off in the recycling. If so, make the effort to find the recycling bin or set one up in your home and discard your item there. Even if it means going to a little more effort, that one action has a huge ripple effect on our environment. For example, recycling one aluminum can saves enough energy to power a computer for three hours!

One thousand five hundred—that's how many plastic water bottles people in the US consume every second! That's pretty mind-blowing, right? And while plastic bottles can be recycled, breaking them down to be reused as another bottle still wastes energy and creates pollution. So, a great habit to get into to support the environment is to stop buying plastic water bottles. Instead, get yourself a reusable aluminum water bottle you can take to school with you daily, so you're not churning through a ton of disposable plastic ones. By not purchasing plastic bottles as often, you're reducing the demand for them, which in turn reduces the number produced. This is significant when you consider that 17 million barrels of oil are used making bottles every year.

Now this habit is one I'm not perfect at (yet), but it's such a helpful one to practice. Whenever you leave an empty room in your home (your cue), get into the habit of switching off the lights. You can also use this protocol with other household appliances, like turning off your air conditioner when you're not around and unplugging electronics, like your TV, phone charger, and printer when you're not using them. Again, these are small actions that, if done daily, can have a significant impact on helping our environment.

Work Hard

It's easy to look at famous and successful people and think how lucky they are compared to us. It seems like they magically had this simple path to get to what they wanted. In today's age of social media where everyone is posting their highlight reels, it really does look like success should happen instantly and effortlessly for us if it's really meant to be.

But if you dig beneath success stories, you'll see that's very rarely the case. For example, J. K. Rowling was rejected by 12 publishers before someone would publish *Harry Potter*. Even when I first started out speaking in high schools, I only got eight school bookings out of 600 emails, and it felt like I was never going to make it.

What may look like an overnight success to us is usually a result of many years of training, practice, and persevering through failure, time and time again. That's why one of the best things you can develop is a good work ethic, in which you value giving your best effort and don't expect things to be easy. Without the hard work, you won't have the skills to make the most of an opportunity, and you never know when your opportunity to prove what you're capable of could come around.

Sticking to your goals can be tough, especially when it feels like progress is slow. You may want to avoid putting in the effort, but the truth is you actually have to keep *doing* it. The reality is sometimes our initial attempts will not be good; we'll be off pitch, make mistakes, miss important shots, or overthink things. But with every attempt you make toward your goal, you can lean in and learn something from it, see what worked well and what didn't. Then you can adjust your technique and focus for next time.

The best time to start practicing that attitude is now. There may be subjects you fail, friends who doubt you, employers who overlook you, and opportunities you miss out on. So commit to practicing the mini habits below to develop the mindset of a successful person. Giving your best effort regardless of the outcome is what matters most.

I KNOW I CAN DO HARD
THINGS, BECAUSE . . .

You are far more determined than you may give yourself credit for. A great habit to get into to understand this is to make a daily log of your hard work so you train your brain to celebrate your efforts as much as the outcome.

Each day for the next 90 days, you're going to write out the words "I know I can do hard things, because . . ." Then complete this sentence with one example from your day when you persevered through a challenge or gave something a lot of effort. For example:

- "I know I can do hard things, because I didn't give up on a math problem till I had the answer."
- "I know I can do hard things, because I pushed myself in the team run at practice today."
- "I know I can do hard things, because I put my hand up and asked for help in class today even though I was nervous."

Everyone has bad days. Even top sports stars like Michael Jordan and Serena Williams have played poorly in important matches. That's life! The key to pushing through those moments of shame and frustration is to have the habit of not letting yourself quit on tough days, Instead, recommit to your goal and your "why" that makes the struggle worth it.

When I first started speaking, some of my talks fell flat with the audience. The humiliation would overcome me, and I'd want to give up entirely, but I didn't. Instead, I used it as a reason to double down on my commitment to my goal by reminding myself that I was doing this to honor my sister and experience the thrill of one day achieving my dreams. It's only when things aren't going our way that we feel like quitting. But you then face the long-term discomfort of not seeing how far you could progress and what you could achieve. You can quit, but not on a bad day. Instead, recommit! Tomorrow is a new day to give it your all.

What's something you've felt like quitting lately? Write down why it's worth holding on to and say to yourself, "I recommit to this."

Think of one famous or successful person you really admire, and I can almost guarantee that their success didn't happen overnight or go according to plan. Chances are it involved hard work, hours upon hours of practicing and refining their skills, along with lots of rejection and battling self-doubt. I know that's been the journey for me, and it will likely be the journey for you.

Rather than judging someone's story by what you see on social media and assuming they found success because they were lucky, get into the habit of digging deep and finding out the real story of what it took to get to where they are today. You'll quickly realize that all the hard work you have to put into your progress is just like their story—all a part of the journey!

So pick one celebrated person you admire and google their name plus the words "journey to success." Learn about their real story for inspiration to always dig deep!

Accept Defeat Graciously

It's the feeling of the championship being on the line, but you miss the final shot as the buzzer sounds. It's the feeling of having given your absolute all on stage after hours of dance practice, yet you come in fourth place. It's the feeling of getting up at 5 a.m. for swim practice for months on end, only to be beat by 0.21 seconds. It's the feeling of defeat—and it sucks.

There's no denying that losing after working your absolute hardest doesn't feel great. I don't think that's a bad thing. In fact, I think feeling disappointed is a natural and healthy emotion to have in the face of defeat if you've really given your best. So you don't need to push that feeling away instantly. You do need to know that the feeling is temporary and not let it turn into bitterness toward your opponents, fellow teammates, or coach, and especially not toward yourself.

We do this by understanding that defeat doesn't mean you're a loser or can't do something. It means that this day wasn't your day to win and feel that glory, but it was your day to learn and practice humility—graciously accepting your loss because you know you're not too good to lose. We're human, and that means sometimes we'll fall short. Even celebrities like Michael Phelps and Beyoncé have been defeated. No one is above losing, no matter how skilled they are. It is inevitable that each of us will face defeat and loss along our journey to success, as we define it for ourselves.

Instead of obsessing over what you can't change, focus on what you *can* change: your attitude. Rather than getting angry with yourself or taking your frustration out on your opponents, embrace the growth mindset that we mentioned in the beginning of this book (page 24). Choose to see defeats like these not as threats to be avoided but as opportunities to build your skills, learn new things, and develop your abilities. When you choose to see defeat in this way, that's where you find the determination to keep showing up and giving your full effort in training and practice. Understanding that no matter the outcome on "game day"—whatever it is you're working to achieve—your effort is worth it because you either win or you *learn*.

ALWAYS SHAKE HANDS
AND CONGRATULATE

No matter how unfair you think the umpire's call was or how aggressive another performer may have been, always practice the habit of shaking the opposing team's hands after a match and/or congratulating your fellow competitors on their win. As much as we may dislike losing, we all know how great it feels to win, so don't try to rob that feeling from them by being unkind. Give them their time, as your time will come.

In the meantime, use your defeat as a time to show your true character. It's easy to smile when you're winning. But to still be friendly and supportive when you've lost takes a certain level of grace and humility that may not have helped you win the competition today but will certainly help you win at life. Think of a past defeat that really sucked at the time. Take a moment to reflect on how you would act differently toward your opponents if winning that day was really about who could show the greatest character.

TURN YOUR SETBACKS
INTO A COMEBACK!

To stop your brain from wallowing in frustration and shame over a loss or defeat, get into the habit of reminding yourself that every setback allows for a comeback! (And who doesn't love a good comeback story?) That's where true inspiration comes from—not when you're always winning, but when you turn those losses around and experience success again.

This can only happen when you choose to get future-focused and action-oriented with the intent to learn from your losses and not shame yourself for them. So, allow for the disappointment, but know that better days are ahead if you stay committed to the belief that this loss is only temporary. By recommitting to working hard, you will soon turn this setback into a comeback. Jot down a recent setback you've had and then write down one action step you can take today to begin turning it into a comeback!

When we lose a game or face a defeat, typically our brain likes to argue with the outcome and ask questions of ourselves like "Why did the ref make that call?" or "Why am I so stupid?" or "Why don't I have any luck?" There is absolutely zero upside to dwelling on those thoughts, as they'll keep you spinning in a place of frustration and self-pity.

Instead, get into the habit of flipping the question to be a far more empowering one: "What can I learn from this?" In fact, think of a recent loss you've faced and challenge yourself to write down three helpful things you can learn from that loss. Going forward, do this for every loss you face. Whether it's to double-check your grip next time, better rehearse your lines, or tighten your shoelaces, there's *always* something to be learned from every experience—with the most valuable lessons coming from our losses.

Takeaways

- Refrain from impulsively spending every cent you're given. Be sure to plan ahead and practice budgeting so you can always afford your needs plus have enough for savings!
- When someone does a good deed for you, pay it forward and do a good deed for someone else. It's what keeps this world a kind and generous place.
- We live in such an amazing world, and it's up to us to look after it. Be sure to practice being eco-friendly and prioritize recycling whenever possible.
- The reality is no one's journey to success is easy or straightforward, so choose to value working hard and putting in the effort, even when progress feels slow.
- You don't have to love defeat, but it's important to practice being a gracious loser and learn from your losses so you can turn setbacks into comebacks!

Chapter Eight

THIS IS JUST THE BEGINNING

We're in the final chapter! But I'm not letting this book end without leaving you inspiring words to ignite your fire to commit to new habits and fuel your belief in what you're truly capable of. As confusing and overwhelming as your teen years may feel, they're also such amazing years to lay the foundation for your future success— achieving whatever goals you strive for. No matter what path you choose in life, these habits will serve you well.

Keep Going

Watching YouTube videos of the experts demonstrating the best technique for goal kicking is great for my knowledge, but in order to actually develop my ability, I would have to put that knowledge into practice and start kicking! The same goes for all the awesome life strategies we've explored together in this book. Stay committed to putting them into practice! And not just once or twice—you need to practice them many times, over and over again, for those strategies to turn into automatic habits for you. Our brain rewires itself through repetition, so be patient and stick with it!

You don't have to tackle everything at once. I suggest picking one chapter and diving deep into getting good at doing those habits and then move on to practicing the habits in the next chapter. Take things at your own pace and don't beat yourself up if you slip up or forget to do something. That's a part of the process. I'm still not perfect at all of these habits either. The main thing is that you don't give up. Set yourself little reminders on your phone or sticky notes in places if you need help remembering to practice these new habits. Or better yet, invite your friend to join you on this mission and inspire each other to get through it together!

Why Does This Matter?

We're in the last few pages of this book, and you may still be thinking, "Yeah, but will developing these habits now really make a big difference in my life down the track?" The answer is yes, absolutely.

By repeating the action of writing down what you're grateful for or reminding yourself "I can do hard things," you're strengthening those positive neural pathways in your brain and making an investment toward your future mental health. Every time you drink a glass of water instead of soda or get up and do your five minutes of exercise, you're making an investment in your physical health and helping to make these positive choices easier for your future self. Every time you sit down and write out your schedule or set your alarm to get up on time, you're making an investment in your future career opportunities, because organizational and time-management skills are standouts to employers. Although it can feel frustrating when progress is slow, understand that the point of creating habits isn't to see results right away; it's about benefiting in the future from the choices you make today.

If you sat and watched a plant grow each day, you wouldn't notice a difference from one day to the next, but if you compare day 1 to day 100, that plant would look entirely different. Watch your progress with the same attitude. You're a seed of incredible potential, and watering it daily with these positive mini habits will really help you grow into your best self!

Tracking Your Habits

One way to make these good habits stick is to track them in a way that lets you check off or cross out each day you perform that habit. It feels awesome to cross something out. Our brain literally gets a hit of dopamine from it! And do you remember what motivates your brain to want to repeat an action again and turn it into a habit? Getting a reward for performing that action! So, tracking your habits is a way to feel more motivated to practice the habits as well as keep you accountable. It's fun to see the row of checked boxes begin to grow, and it makes you more committed to wanting to do the habit because you don't want to break the chain and lose momentum!

You can make the habit tracker as fancy or as simple as you like. You can use a piece of paper or a pen or a Word doc or a note-taking app on your phone or computer. Also, if you google "habit tracker," you'll find a ton of free templates you can print and fill out. There are lots of free apps you can download, too, including Habitify, Strides, and HabitHub. I recommend you put your tracker somewhere obvious—like on your bedroom wall or home screen of your phone—as you can use it as a cue to do the habit, and it can be inspiring to see the progress you're making with it.

The Last Word

Congratulations! You've officially reached the end of this book and begun a whole new journey of building the path to your greatest success in life through the practice of these mini habits. No doubt the path will get rocky at times, as life will always be filled with unexpected challenges, but know that you always have these habits to support you during tough times. Personally, the habit of gratitude and paying it forward carried me through the dark days of grief just after losing my sister. The habits of conflict resolution, such as hearing others out and not making things personal, have helped me save relationships very important to me. Know that no matter what's happening in your day, these habits are here for you to help make all of these things that much easier to navigate.

Remember, it's not about doing these habits perfectly but persistently. Don't forget to have some fun with them, too! One of the biggest mistakes I made as a teen was taking myself too seriously and putting so much pressure on myself. So if I could give you one word of advice, it would be to lighten up and find the humor in things when you can. If you slip up or make a mistake, have a laugh and move on to the next day.

Finally, I know it feels like your teen years will never end, but they do and far quicker than you think. Instead of waiting around to do something to prepare yourself for what's to come next, start today by committing to the habits I've carefully handpicked for you in this book. When you combine these habits, they'll help you live a happier, more resilient, and fulfilling life. They are my gift to you that you can then give as a gift to your future self to feel so proud of who you've become.

Although I can't be there to motivate you through these habits every day, this book is here for you anytime you want some extra encouragement or guidance. I'm on your team and cheering you on always! Now go and get practicing. Your growth is in your hands!

RESOURCES

To learn more about building good habits for life:

Atomic Habits: Tiny Changes, Remarkable Results by James Clear

Focus & Thrive: Executive Functioning Strategies for Teens by Laurie Chaikind McNulty

Tiny Habits: The Small Changes That Change Everything by BJ Fogg

For a deeper dive into some of the key areas we've touched on in this book, like changing your mindset, managing your emotions, and building your self-esteem:

Good Thinking: A Teenager's Guide to Managing Stress and Emotion Using CBT by Sarah Edelman and Louise Remond

The Happiest Man on Earth by Eddie Jaku

How to Adult, A Practical Guide: Advice on Living, Loving, Working, and Spending Like a Grown-Up by Jamie Goldstein

The Mindfulness Journal for Teens: Prompts and Practices to Help You Stay Cool, Calm, and Present by Jennie Marie Battistin

Mindset: Changing The Way You Think to Fulfil Your Potential by Carol Dweck

The Teen's Guide to Social Skills: Practical Advice for Building Empathy, Confidence, and Self-Esteem by Kate Fitzsimons

What Do You Stand For? For Teens: A Guide to Building Character by Barbara A. Lewis

APPS

For getting cues to do your habits and track your progress:

Habitify (Habitify.me)

The HabitHub (TheHabitHub.com)

Strides (StridesApp.com)

For helping you manage your stress through meditation and relaxation:

Calm: Guided meditations, sleep stories, breathing programs, and relaxing music (Calm.com)

Insight Timer: Guided meditations and talks by meditation and mindfulness experts, psychologists, and teachers (InsightTimer.com)

For helping you with budgeting and saving money:

Bankaroo: Created by an 11-year-old back in 2011, this app will teach you how to better manage your allowance, gifts, and chore money using a fun, gamified interface. (Bankaroo.com)

BusyKid: Used together with your parents or guardian, this app teaches you all the money management skills you need to develop a good work ethic so you're better prepared for the future. (BusyKid.com)

For helping you with practicing gratitude and self-love:

ThinkUp: A great app for motivation and confidence, with a reminder feature that pops up positive affirmations on your phone daily. (ThinkUp.me)

I Am - Positive Affirmations: This app sends you notifications of positive messages throughout the day to encourage you to practice positive thinking. (MonkeyTaps.net)

For helping you with time management and organizational skills:

myHomework Student Planner: This app has a calendar where you can track your upcoming assignments, projects, exams, and other important events, and gives you the ability to sync your assignments and get reminders for when they're due so you never miss a due date! (MyHomeworkApp.com)

Remember the Milk: An awesome place to host your to-do list. You'll receive reminders via email and text for an upcoming task so you're no longer forgetting important things that need to get done. (RememberTheMilk.com)

SOCIAL MEDIA

Kate Gladdin, International Resilience Speaker and Certified LCS Life Coach for Teens (@kategladdin)

KnowingUP: Teen Life Coaching, Certified LCS Life Coach (@thelifecoachforteengirls)

Joey Mascio, Certified LCS Life Coach for Teens and Young Adults (@joey_firmlyfoundedcoaching)

PODCASTS

Okay. Now What? with Kate Gladdin: Yes, I have my own podcast! Be sure to check it out so you can keep listening and learning along with me. I think you'll especially love Episode 92, called "Finding Motivation to Do Something You Don't Want to Do."

Secrets for an Awesome Life with Joey Mascio

The Teen Life Coach with Sami Halvorsen

REFERENCES

Adler, Lana. "How to Go to Sleep Earlier." Sleep.org. Updated November 20, 2020. Sleep.org/train-go-sleep-earlier.

Better Health Channel. "Teenagers and Communication." Accessed January 30, 2021. BetterHealth.vic.gov.au /health/healthyliving/teenagers-and-communication.

Blanco, Lydia T. "5 Key Budgeting Basics for Teens." *Today*. February 1, 2020. Today.com/parenting-guides/five-key -budgeting-basics-t177200.

Caring for Kids. "Teens and Sleep: Why It's Important and How to Get More of It." Accessed January 17, 2021. www.CaringforKids.cps.ca/handouts/healthy-living /teens_and_sleep.

Chernoff, Angel. "60 Selfless Ways to Pay It Forward." Charter for Compassion. Accessed February 10, 2021. CharterforCompassion.org/practicing-peace/60-selfless -ways-to-pay-it-forward.

Christian, Lyn. "The 4 Communication Styles: How Behavioral Traits Affect Communication." SoulSalt. August 22, 2019. SoulSalt.com/communication-style/#:~:text =Communication%20styles%20are%20the%20broad,the %20quality%20of%20your%20relationships.

Clear, James. "How to Start New Habits That Actually Stick." JamesClear.com. Accessed December 7, 2020. JamesClear.com/three-steps-habit-change.

Cooper, Belle. "How to Ruthlessly Prioritize Tasks to Get More Done." Zapier. May 13, 2019. Zapier.com /blog/prioritize-task-list-methods.

Dewi, Dinar Sari Eka, and Hazaliza Binti Hamzah. "The Relationship between Spirituality, Quality of Life, and Resilience." *Advances in Social Science, Education and Humanities Research* 349 (October 2019): 145–47. doi.org/10.2991/iccd-19.2019.39.

Duckworth, Angela. *Grit: The Power of Passion and Perseverance.* New York: Scribner, 2016.

Duhigg, Charles. "How Habits Work." CharlesDuhigg.com. Accessed December 12, 2020. CharlesDuhigg.com /how-habits-work.

Economy, Peter. "7 Super Effective Ways to Make Kindness a Habit." *Inc.* Accessed February 7, 2021. Inc.com /peter-economy/7-remarkably-effective-ways-to-make -kindness-a-habit.html.

The Environmentor (blog). "Were There More Trees 100 Years Ago vs Today?" Tentree. Accessed February 10, 2021. Blog.tentree.com/fact-check-are-there-really -more-trees-today-than-100-years-ago.

Erich, Darlene. "3 Benefits of Washing Face with Cold Water." V10PlusUSA. September 19, 2019. V10PlusUSA.com/blogs /news/3-benefits-of-washing-face-with-cold-water.

Gregoire, Carolyn. "5 Amazing Things Your Brain Does While You Sleep." HuffPost. Updated September 29, 2014. HuffPost.com/entry/brain-sleep-_n_5863736.

Harford, MJ. "3 Breathing Exercises to Help Reduce Stress and Anxiety." Sunstone Counseling. December 18, 2018. SunstoneCounselors.com/3-breathing-exercises-to -help-reduce-stress-and-anxiety.

Hauser, Elyse. "Why You Remember Things Better When You Write Them Down." LifeSavvy. March 3, 2020. LifeSavvy.com/19204/why-you-remember-things -better-when-you-write-them-down.

Hussein, Jennifer. "Subtle Signs Your Quarantine Diet Will Do Lasting Damage." Eat This, Not That! May 13, 2020. EatThis.com/signs-of-a-bad-diet.

Jacob. "10 Tips on Budgeting for Teens in 2021." *Teen Financial Freedom* (blog). August 4, 2020. TeenFinancialFreedom.com/10-tips-on-budgeting -for-teens.

Jiang, Jingjing. "Teens Who Are Constantly Online Are Just As Likely to Socialize with Their Friends Offline." Pew Research Center. November 28, 2018. PewResearch.org /fact-tank/2018/11/28/teens-who-are-constantly-online -are-just-as-likely-to-socialize-with-their-friends-offline.

Johnson, Charlotte. "Did You Know That Most Emotions Last 90 Seconds?" Care Counseling. Accessed December 27, 2020. Care-Clinics.com/did-you-know -that-most-emotions-last-90-seconds.

Kloppers, Mandy. "Unsociable Teenagers." MentalHelp.net. Accessed February 4, 2021. MentalHelp.net/blogs /unsociable-teenagers.

Kuczyńska, Dominika. "Short Story about the Brain Chem-icals and How They Affect Players." Daft Mobile. December 23, 2016. Blog.DaftMobile.com/short-story -about-the-brain-chemicals-and-how-they-affect -players-d078792139ec.

Kukolic, Siobhan Kelleher. "Between Stimulus and and Response There is a Space." Thrive Global. January 27, 2020. ThriveGlobal.com/stories/between-stimulu s-and-response-there-is-a-space/#:~:text=Viktor %20Frankl%2C%20an%20Austrian%20neurologist,our %20growth%20and%20our%20freedom.%E2%80%9D.

Lierman, Kaci. "5 Reasons to Get a Workout Buddy: Motivation and Accountability." *NIFS Healthy Living Blog*. February 15, 2018. NIFS.org/blog/five-reasons-to-find-a-workout -buddy-motivation-accountability-and-more.

Lim, Teddy. "Habit Hack: The Science Behind How a Habit Is Formed." Lifehack. Accessed December 7, 2020. Lifehack.org/articles/lifestyle/habit-hack-the-science -behind-how-habit-formed.html.

Lindberg, Sarah, and Erin Kelly. "Your Anxiety Loves Sugar. Eat These 3 Things Instead." Healthline. June 23, 2020. Healthline.com/health/mental-health/how-sugar -harms-mental-health#depression-risk.

Matsumoto, David, and Hyi Sung Hwang. "Reading Facial Expressions of Emotion." American Psychological Association. May 2011. APA.org/science/about/psa/2011/05 /facial-expressions#:~:text=Thus%20there%20is %20strong%20evidence,surprise%20(see%20Figure%201).

McDonald, Juliana. "Curbing America's Trash Production: Statistics and Solutions." Dumpsters.com. April 29, 2020. Dumpsters.com/blog/us-trash-production.

McGinley, Karson. "The Correlation between Spirituality and Happiness." Chopra. August 29, 2018. Chopra.com /articles/the-correlation-between-spirituality -and-happiness.

Monroe, Heather. "The Importance of Sleep for Teen Mental Health." U.S. News & World Report. July 2, 2018. Health.USNews.com/health-care/for-better /articles/2018-07-02/the-importance-of-sleep-for -teen-mental-health.

Monroe, Jamison, Jr. "Get Moving: The Benefits of Exercise for Teen Mental Health." U.S. News & World Report. May 28, 2018. Health.USNews.com/health-care/for-better /articles/2018-05-28/get-moving-the-benefits-of -exercise-for-teen-mental-health.

Murphy, Coner. "How You Can Have Successful Habits in 3 Easy Steps!" *The Positopian* (blog). September 9, 2017. Medium.com/the-positopian/how-you-can-have -successful-habits-in-3-easy-steps-fc548d3ae4ee.

Nield, David. "Even Just Seeing Your Phone Nearby Can Mess with Your Brain Power." ScienceAlert. June 27, 2017. ScienceAlert.com/even-just-having-your -phone-in-view-reduces-your-brain-power -says-a-new-study#:~:text=Even%20Just%20Seeing %20Your%20Phone%20Nearby%20Can%20Mess%20With %20Your%20Brain%20Power,-DAVID%20NIELD&text =According%20to%20the%20team%20from,try %20not%20to%20be%20distracted.

Not Quite an Adult (blog). "Budgeting for Teens: A 6 Step Guide." January 10, 2019. NotQuiteAnAdult.com /budgeting-for-teens.

Nunez, Kirsten, and Karen Lamoreux. "What Is the Purpose of Sleep?" Healthline. July 20, 2020. Healthline.com /health/why-do-we-sleep.

Oxford Learner's Dictionaries. "Body language." Accessed December 28, 2020. OxfordLearnersDictionaries.com /us/definition/english/body-language.

Pacheco, Danielle. "The Best Temperature for Sleep." Sleep Foundation. Updated October 29, 2020. SleepFoundation.org/bedroom-environment /best-temperature-for-sleep#:~:text=The%20best %20bedroom%20temperature%20for,for%20the%20most %20comfortable%20sleep.

Park, Alice. "Teens Are Just As Sedentary As 60 Year Olds."
  Time. June 16, 2017. Time.com/4821963/teens-sedentary
  -lifestyle-exercise.

Patterson, Ransom. "The 11 Best Habit Tracking Apps in
  2021." College Info Geek. Updated January 21, 2021.
  CollegeInfoGeek.com/habit-tracker.

Pink, Daniel H. "The Power of Habits—and the Power
  to Change Them." Daniel H. Pink. Accessed December 6,
  2020. DanPink.com/2012/03/the-power-of-habits
  -and-the-power-to-change-them.

Price-Mitchell, Marilyn. "Youth Mentoring Rocks! How
  Teens Find Great Mentors." Roots of Action. June 19,
  2019. RootsOfAction.com/youth-mentoring.

Raising Children Network (Australia). "Sleep and Teenagers:
  12-18 Years." Updated May 19, 2020. RaisingChildren.net
  .au/teens/healthy-lifestyle/sleep/sleep-teens.

Raising Children Network (Australia). "Teenage Friends and
  Friendships." Accessed February 4, 2021. RaisingChildren
  .net.au/pre-teens/behaviour/peers-friends-trends
  /teen-friendships.

Sack, David. "4 Ways Sugar Could Be Harming Your Mental
  Health." Psychology Today. September 2, 2013.
  PsychologyToday.com/us/blog/where-science
  -meets-the-steps/201309/4-ways-sugar-could
  -be-harming-your-mental-health.

Scholtus, Petz. "The US Consumes 1500 Plastic Water
  Bottles Every Second, a Fact by Watershed." Treehugger.
  Updated May 12, 2020. Treehugger.com/the-us
  -consumes-plastic-water-bottles-every-second
  -a-fact-by-watershed-4858111.

Shortsleeve, Cassie. "4 Ways to Set a Bedtime Routine for Teenagers." Saatva. September 8, 2020. Saatva .com/blog/bedtime-routine-for-teenagers.

Society for Personality and Social Psychology. "How We Form Habits, Change Existing Ones." ScienceDaily. August 8, 2014. ScienceDaily.com/releases/2014 /08/140808111931.htm.

Solara Mental Health. "Water, Depression, and Anxiety." Accessed January 19, 2021. SolaraMentalHealth.com /can-drinking-enough-water-help-my-depression -and-anxiety.

Stempel, Justin. "Calculate How Many Bottles of Water You Need." H2O Coolers. March 30, 2020. H2OCoolers .com/news/healthy-lifestyle/how-many-bottles-of -water-should-i-drink-per-day/#:~:text=Well%2C %20the%20typical%20size%20bottle,water%20is%2016.9 %20fluid%20ounces.

Stevenson, Sarah. "There's Magic in Your Smile." Psychology Today. June 25, 2012. PsychologyToday.com/us /blog/cutting-edge-leadership/201206/there-s-magic -in-your-smile.

Twenge, Jean. "Teens Have Less Face Time with Their Friends – and Are Lonelier Than Ever." The Conversation. Accessed February 4, 2021. TheConversation.com /teens-have-less-face-time-with-their-friends-and -are-lonelier-than-ever-113240.

Van Dijk, Sheri. "Say WHAT? Helping Teens Communicate Effectively." Charlotte Parent. July 27, 2011. CharlotteParent.com/say-what-helping-teens -communicate-effectively.

Wealthy Gorilla. "7 Reasons to Start Tracking Your Habits."
Accessed February 13, 2021. WealthyGorilla.com
/7-reasons-start-tracking-your-habits.

Weir, Karessa. "The Benefits of Friendship." MSU Today.
Accessed February 5, 2021. MSUToday.msu.edu
/news/2020/the-benefits-of-friendship.

Wignall, Nick. "Emotional Vulnerability: What It Is and Why
It Matters." NickWignall.com. May 18, 2020. NickWignall
.com/emotional-vulnerability.

Yardney, Michael. "Six Famous People Who Failed Before
Succeeding." Property Update. March 18, 2020.
PropertyUpdate.com.au/six-famous-people-who
-failed-before-succeeding.

INDEX

Acknowledgments

I wholeheartedly want to thank Callisto Media for the opportunity to write another book that helps fulfill my mission of empowering teens to live happier and healthier lives! To my wonderful partner, Nate, thank you for being my rock throughout this writing process and my life journey—every day is better with you in it. I also want to give a shout-out to my amazing friends and family who continue to cheer me on and believe in me no matter what. Finally, to my sister Nicole, I will continue to live life large enough for the both of us, always.

About the Author

 From a broken-hearted sister battling an eating disorder to one of Australia's "100 Women of Influence," **Kate Gladdin** (née Fitzsimons) is living proof that what doesn't kill us can make us stronger. She is an international youth speaker, teen resilience coach, and author of *The Teen's Guide to Social Skills*.

Through her school talks, online coaching programs, and podcast, *Okay. Now What?*, Kate has a unique ability to connect with teens that's helped more than 200,000 students build resilience in a way they've described as "life changing." Originally from Sydney, Australia, Kate now lives happily in the United States with her partner, Nate Gladdin. Her favorite things include homemade pizza and playing in the snow with her dog, Jaku.